No-Glamour® Question Structure
Wh- Questions

by Andrea M. Lazzari

Skills	**Ages**
■ formulating questions	■ 7 and up
■ written language	**Grades**
	■ 2 and up

Evidence-Based Practice

- Grammar, discourse structure, and metalinguistics are all connected to reading/writing achievement and are required for text comprehension.[1]

- Graphic and semantic organizers, question generation, and summarization are three strategies that have a firm scientific basis for improving comprehension.[2]

- Children with expressive language disorders frequently have problems developing literacy skills and require specific instruction to acquire reading and writing skills.[3]

- Students should understand specific grammar structures before they are asked to use them in speech.[3]

- Both comprehension and production should be considered in all areas of grammar. Particular attention should be paid to syntactic movement, especially *wh-* questions.[3]

The activities in this book incorporate the above principles and are also based on expert professional practice.

References

[1] American Speech-Language-Hearing Association (ASHA). 2001. *Roles and responsibilities of speech-language pathologists with respect to reading and writing in children and adolescents.* Available from www.asha.org/docs/html/GL2001-00062.html

[2] National Reading Panel Report. 2000. *Teaching children to read: An evidence-based assessment of the scientific research literature on reading and its implications for reading instruction.* www.readingrockets.org/research/federal

[3] Royal College of Speech & Language Therapists (RCSLT). 2005. *Clinical guidelines for speech and language therapists.* www.rcslt.org/resources/clinicalguidelines

LinguiSystems®

LinguiSystems, Inc.
3100 4th Avenue
East Moline, IL 61244
800-776-4332

FAX: 800-577-4555
E-mail: service@linguisystems.com
Web: linguisystems.com

Copyright © 2008 LinguiSystems, Inc.

All of our products are copyrighted to protect the fine work of our authors. You may only copy the student materials as needed for your own use. Any other reproduction or distribution of the pages in this book is prohibited, including copying the entire book to use as another primary source or "master" copy.

Printed in the U.S.A.
ISBN 978-0-7606-0795-4

About the Author

Andrea M. Lazzari, Ed.D., is a speech-language pathologist for Henrico County Public Schools in Richmond, Virginia. She has also worked in a community clinic and in private practice. She has taught preschool students with disabilities and was Supervisor of Early Childhood Special Education Programs for the state of Virginia. She has also served as a teacher trainer at the college and university levels. *No-Glamour Question Structure: Wh- Questions* is Andrea's twenty-fifth publication with LinguiSystems. She is the author or co-author of numerous other publications, including *No-Glamour Question Structure: Interrogative Reversals, Vocabulary To Go, 125 Ways to Be a Better Test Taker–Elementary, 125 Ways to Be a Better Test Taker–Intermediate,* and the *HELP* series.

Dedication

With thanks to my team members Karen Stontz for her patient editing and Margaret Warner for her wonderful illustrations

Table of Contents

Introduction 4

Picture Symbol Key 6

Units

    Who Questions 7

    Where Questions 32

    When Questions 57

    What Questions 82

    Why Questions 107

    How Questions 132

Wrap-Up 157

Introduction

The language used by teachers and students in their classrooms has a significant impact on what is learned. Active participation in classroom activities (including question-and-answer exchanges) increases students' access to learning and improves their long-term educational outcomes. Students who lack communicative competence in the classroom may experience educational failure because they do not have equal access to the curriculum (Wilkinson & Silliman, 2000).

No-Glamour Question Structure: Wh- Questions is written to help students gain fuller access to the curriculum. It is a straightforward, picture-based program to help students formulate questions, enabling them to participate more actively in question-and-answer exchanges in their classrooms. The target audience for this book is students ages seven and older with oral and written language deficits, including young students with language delays, older students whose written language is significantly weaker than their oral language, students whose second language is English, and students with autism. These students often have particular difficulty formulating relevant questions using correct word order. It is recommended that students have the prerequisite skill of producing a variety of statements incorporating present progressive verbs and auxiliaries with singular and plural nouns and pronouns before beginning the tasks in this volume.

Each unit begins with a list of 20 target questions and a modeling script to teach the format to the student. Within each unit, questions are grouped in a hierarchy of difficulty. Two picture sequences are presented on each of the following 20 pages in the unit. The first picture sequence presents a statement. The second picture sequence elicits a question about the previous statement (e.g., "The girl is happy" elicits the question "Who is happy?"). Each of the question picture sequences begins with a large question symbol containing the initial question word (Who, Where, When, etc.). Some students may need verbal cues for the question words.

If the primary goal of intervention is oral language, the student can dictate responses to be written in each blank. When the student becomes proficient in formulating the questions aloud, you can elicit a written response from him.

Verb tenses for stimulus items can be easily changed to reflect an individual student's goals. Adjectives can be incorporated to make the tasks more difficult. Copies of the stimulus pictures can be colored to elicit adjectives within the questions. Students may also add adjectives and adverbs not pictured in the illustrations.

Introduction, continued

Both nouns and pronouns are used in the stimulus items. These may also be changed as needed. A picture symbol key of the pronoun symbols is presented on page 6. It will be helpful to familiarize students with these symbols before beginning the units.

A review is provided at the end of each unit. Each review presents one stimulus picture for each of the 20 practice items in the unit. The student is asked to formulate questions beginning with specific question words. The student is not expected to repeat the questions verbatim as stated or written on the previous practice sheets. Any relevant, grammatically correct question beginning with the target word is acceptable.

The Wrap-Up section at the end of the book presents ten new stimulus pictures. Beneath each picture, four initial question words are presented. The goal is for the student to formulate novel questions beginning with each of the target words. There are no expected correct responses to these items. Rather, it is an opportunity for students to creatively formulate a variety of questions. This section also provides a natural carryover to question formulation using pictures from other sources.

The ultimate goal of *No-Glamour Question Structure: Wh- Questions* is for students to develop competence in question formulation, enabling them to use these forms naturally in their classrooms and when interacting with peers at school. Students who need additional practice in question formulation may benefit from the companion volume for formulating questions, *No-Glamour Question Structure: Interrogative Reversals*.

I hope you will find this volume easy-to-use and effective in helping your students develop skills in question formulation.

Andrea

Wilkinson, L.C., & Silliman, E.R. (2000). Classroom language and literacy learning. In M.L. Kamil, P.B. Mosenthal, P.D. Pearson, & R. Barr, (Eds.), *Handbook of reading research: Vol. III*. Mahwah, NJ: Lawrence Erlbaum Associates.

Picture Symbol Key

Who Questions

1. Who is happy?
2. Who is muddy?
3. Who is proud?
4. Who is wet?
5. Who is sleeping?
6. Who is clapping?
7. Who can hop?
8. Who may have some water?
9. Who will kick the soccer ball?
10. Who will pass out the test?
11. Who will open the gate?
12. Who can lift the heavy box?
13. Who can reach the top shelf?
14. Who is sitting in the rocking chair?
15. Who is knocking on the door?
16. Who is looking for the Frisbee?
17. Who is standing behind the fence?
18. Who is dancing on the stage?
19. Who will rest on the grass?
20. Who will march on the field?

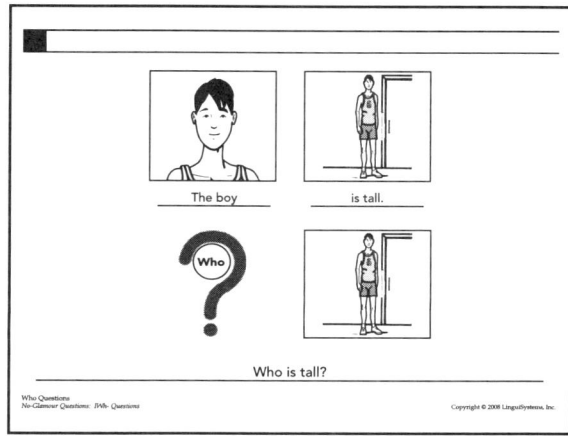

Modeling Script:

1. Look at the pictures at the top of the page. Let's point to the pictures and tell what is happening. **The boy is tall.**
2. Now look at the pictures at the bottom of the page. When you see this big question mark, you start with the question word inside the circle. This word is **who**.
3. Now let's ask the whole question while we point to each picture. **Who is tall?**
4. Now let's write the words under each picture. Remember, a written question ends with a question mark.

Who Questions

The girl

is happy.

Who?

1

2

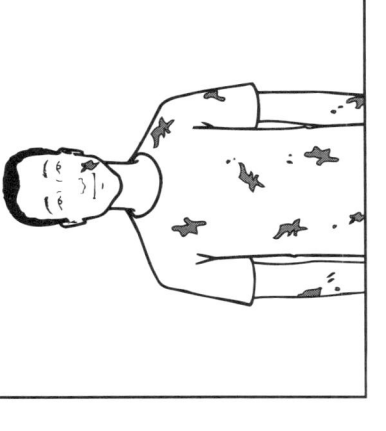 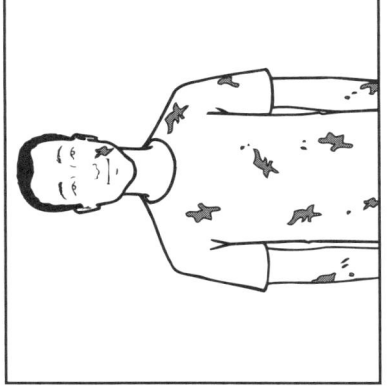

The man _____ is muddy.

Who Questions
No-Glamour Question Structure: Wh- Questions

The girl _____ is proud.

4

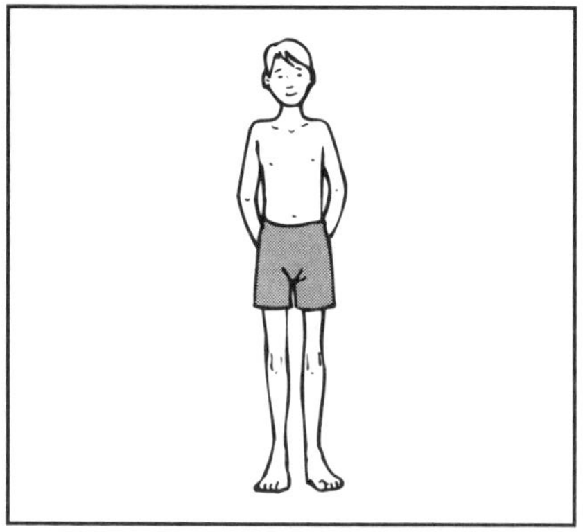

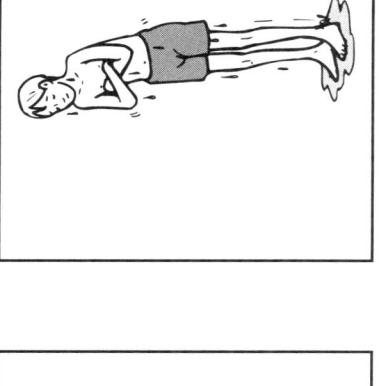

The swimmer

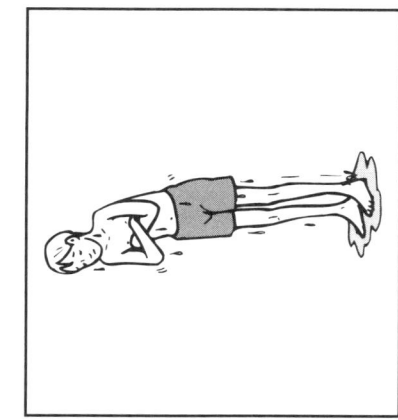

is wet.

Who ?

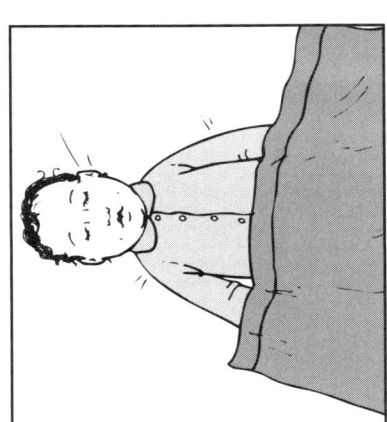 

_____ is sleeping.

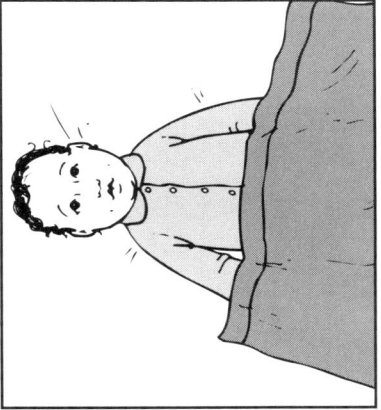

The baby _____

Who Questions

Kim

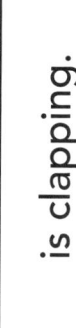 is clapping.

Who?

Who Questions

The boys

can hop.

Who Questions

may have some water.

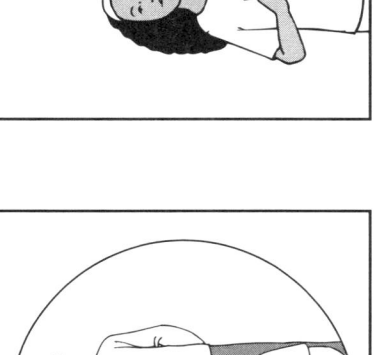

Everyone

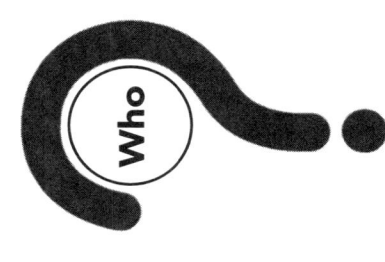

Who?

9

Mary will kick the soccer ball.

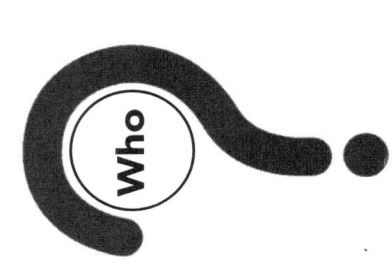

10

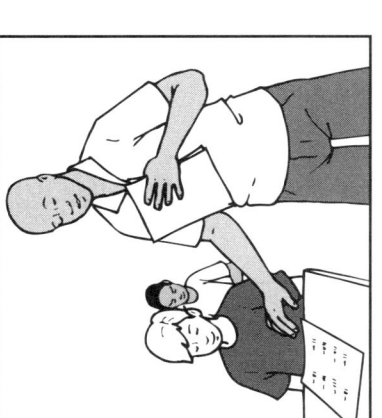 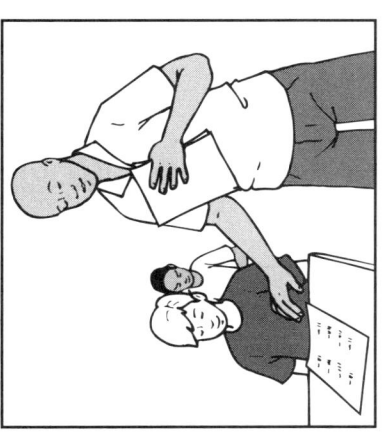 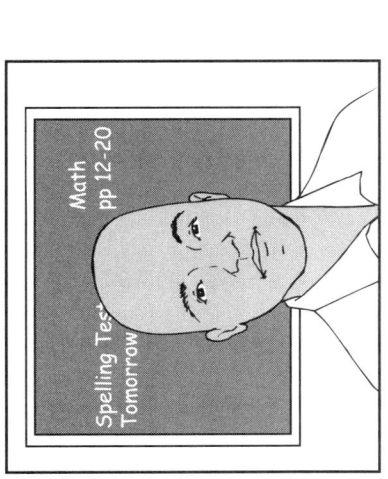

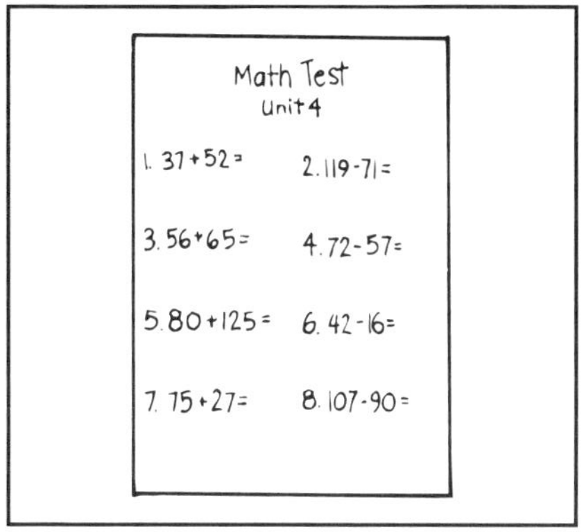

The teacher | will pass out | the test.

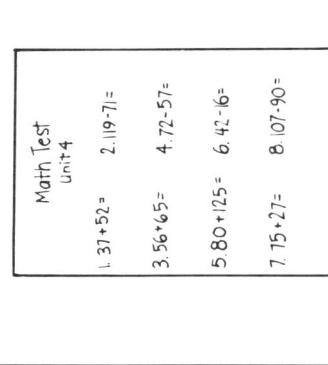 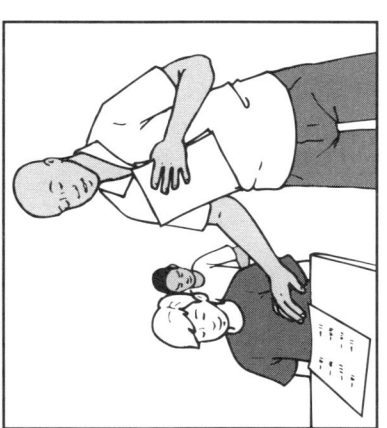

11

Joe | will open | the gate.

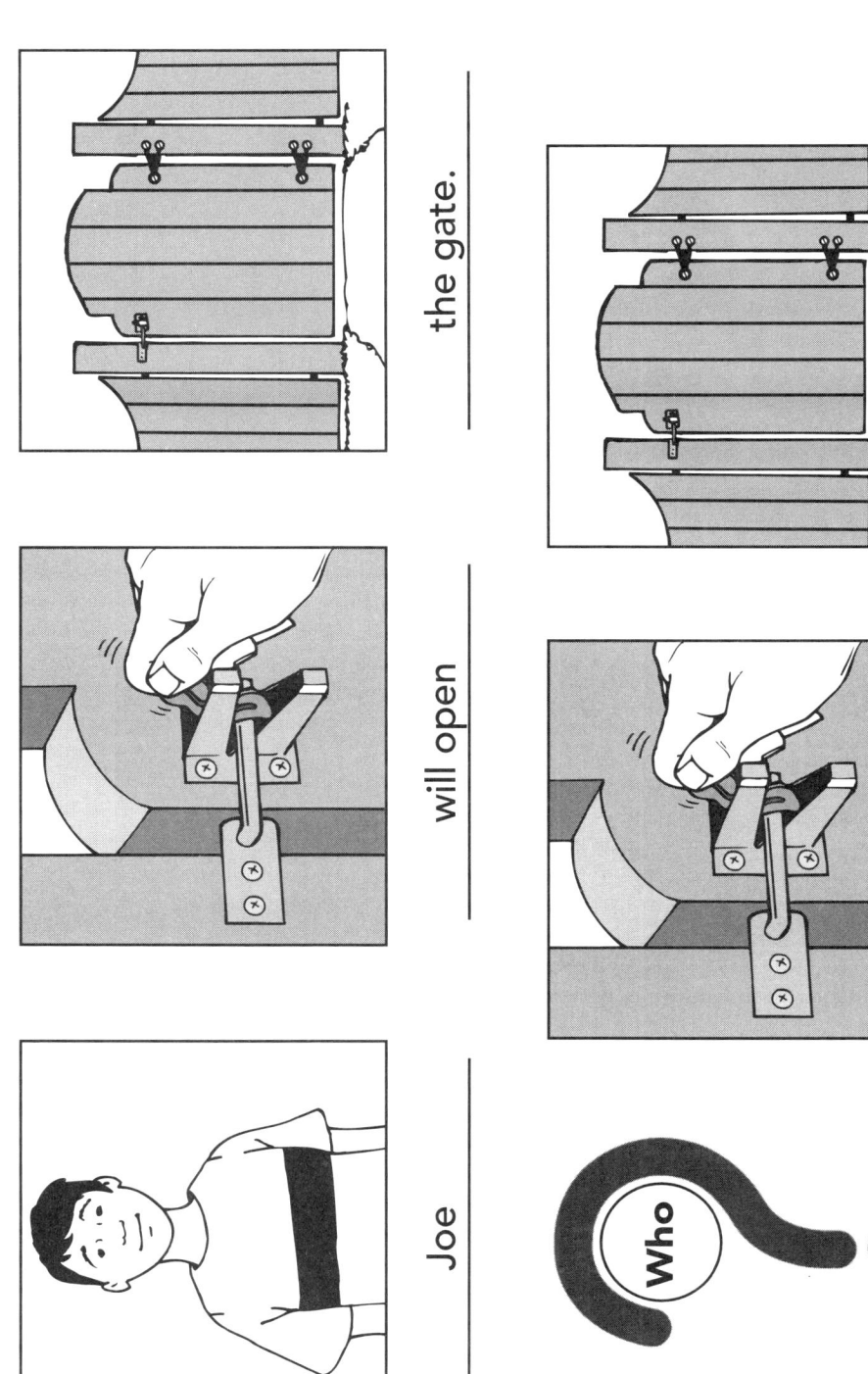

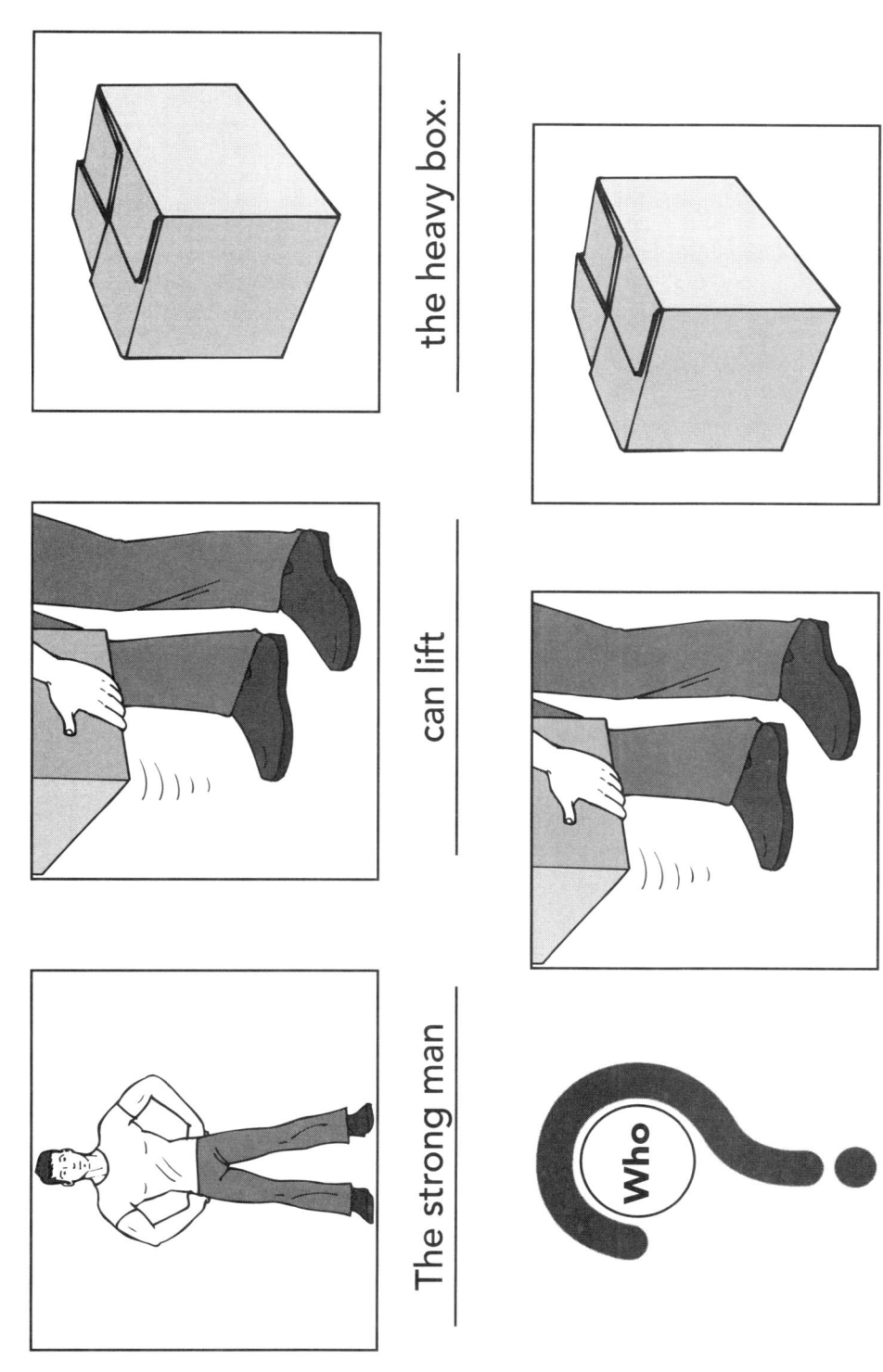

The strong man _____ can lift _____ the heavy box.

Who ?

13

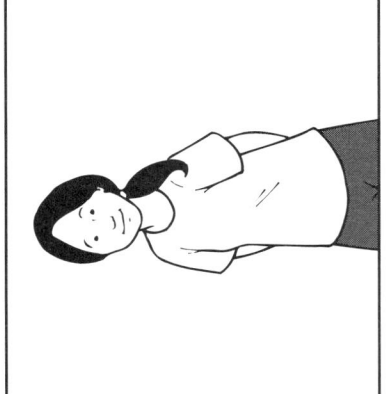

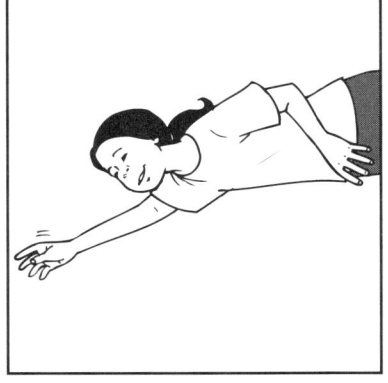

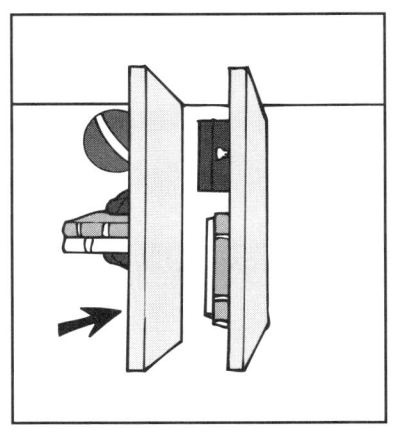

The girl can reach the top shelf.

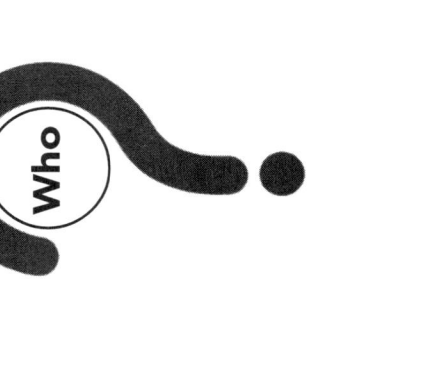

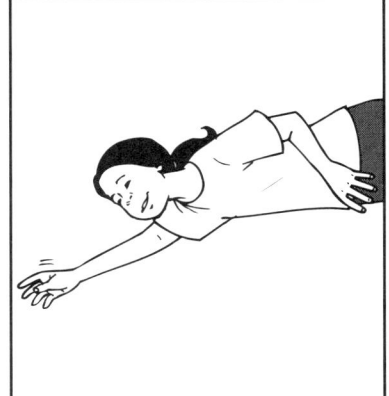

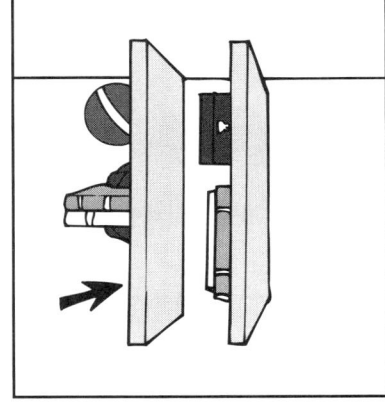

14

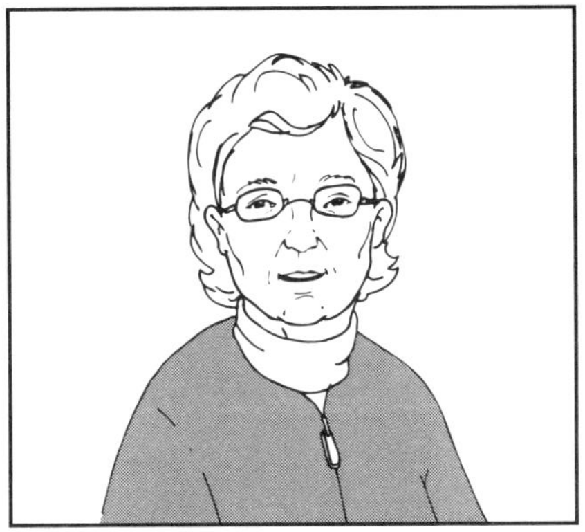

Grandma

is sitting

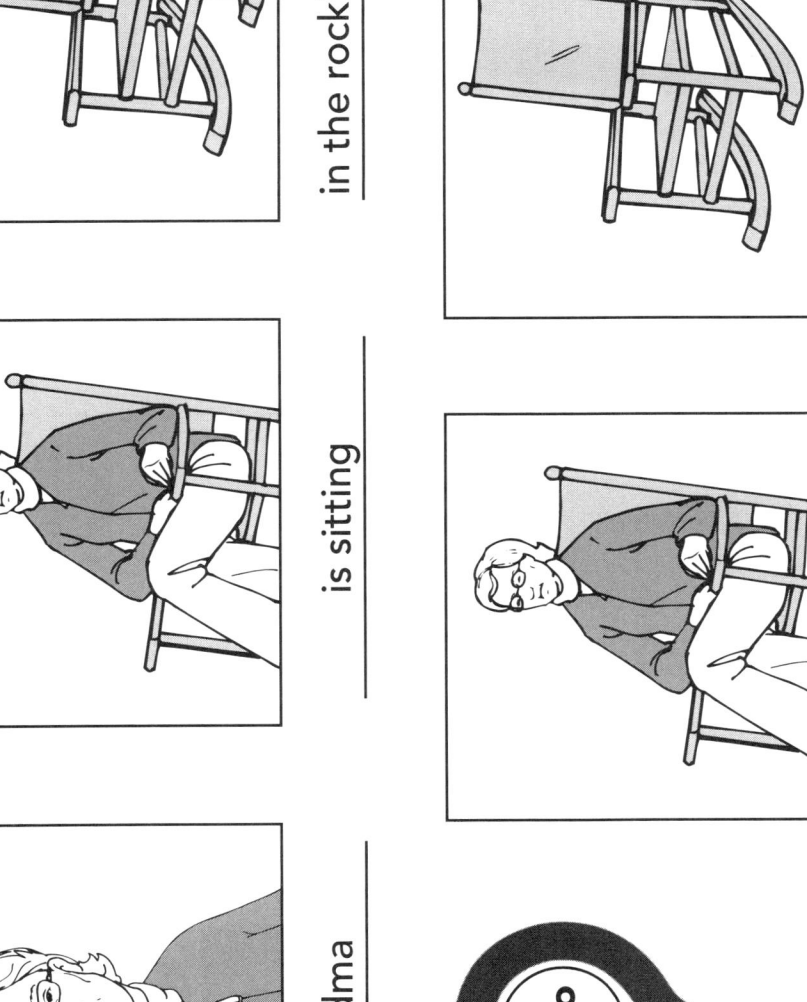

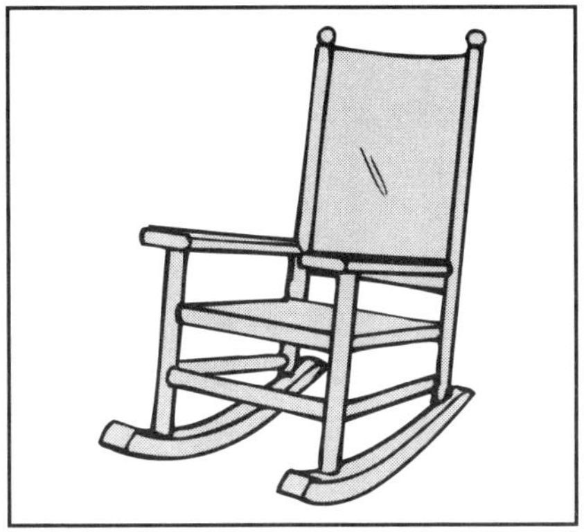

in the rocking chair.

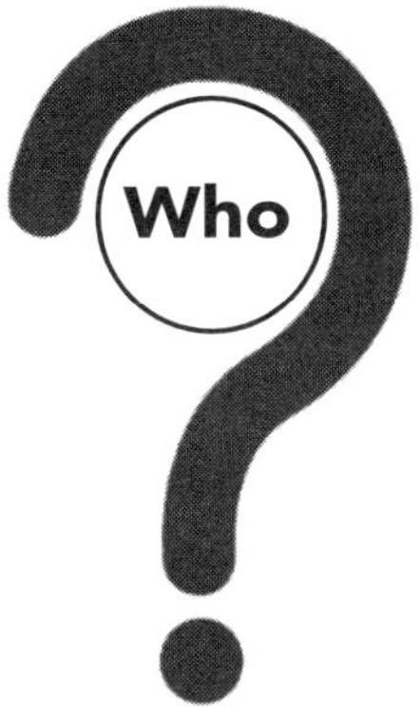

16

Luke is looking for the Frisbee.

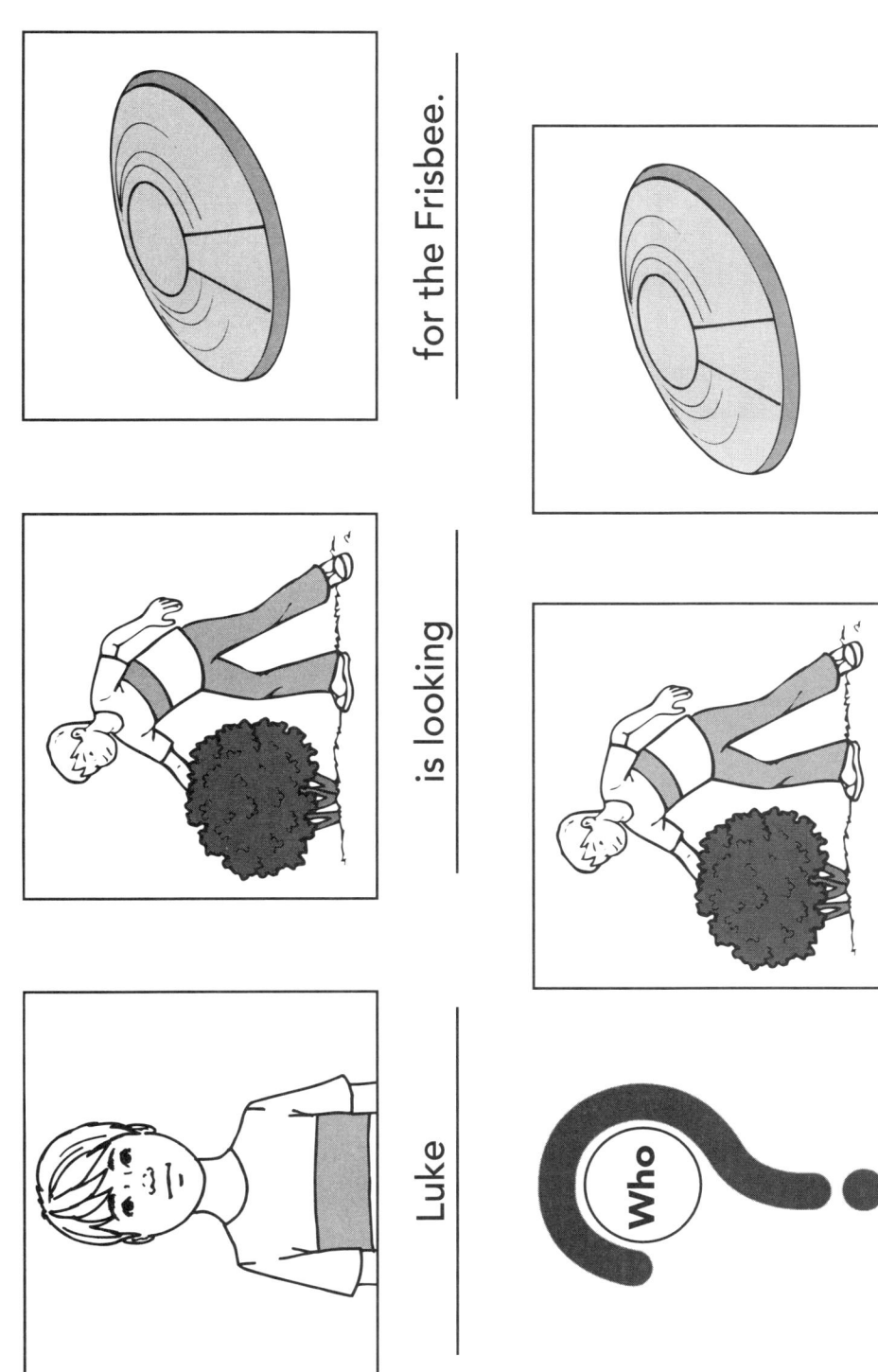

17

The girl

is standing

behind the fence.

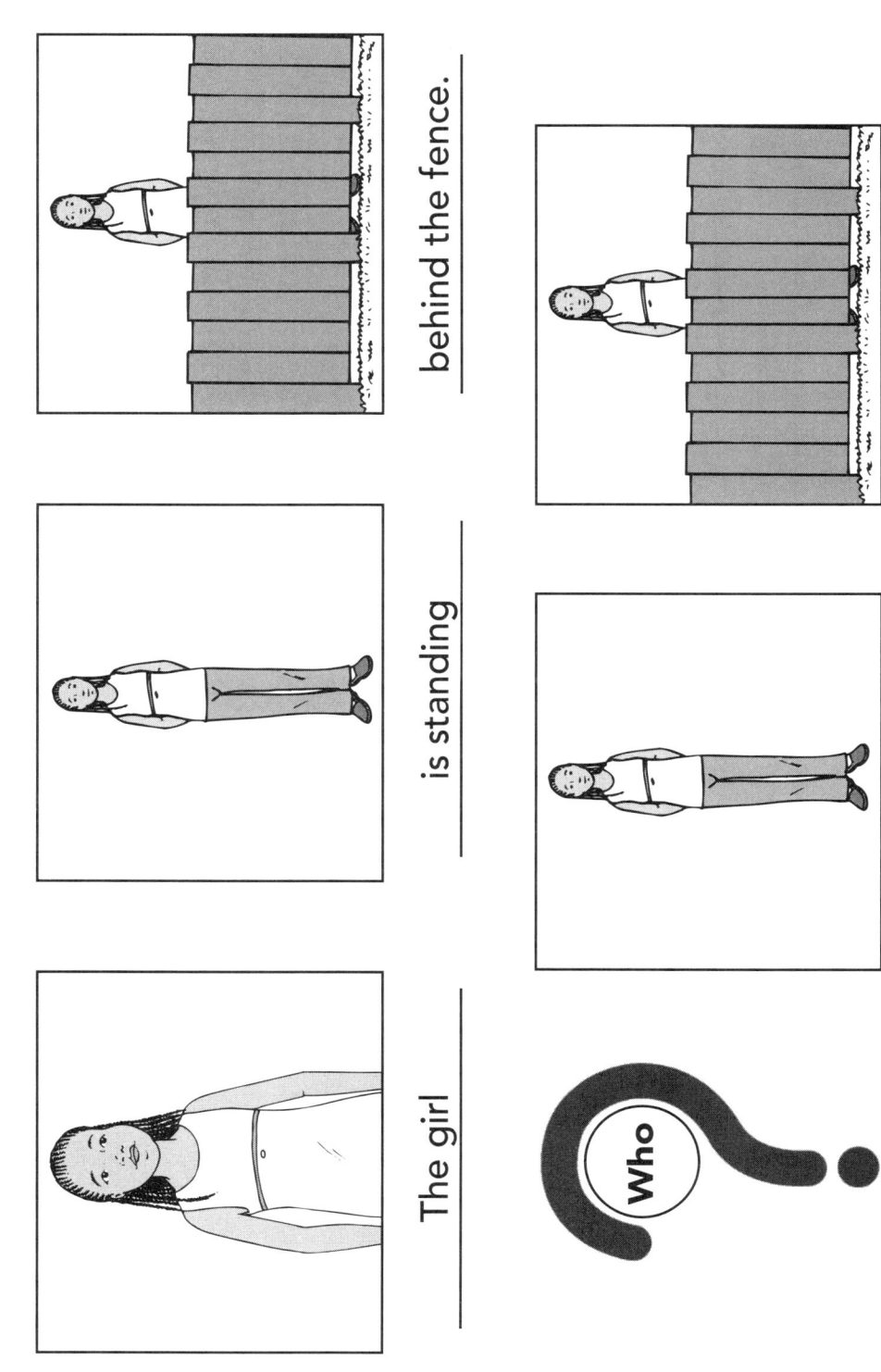

18

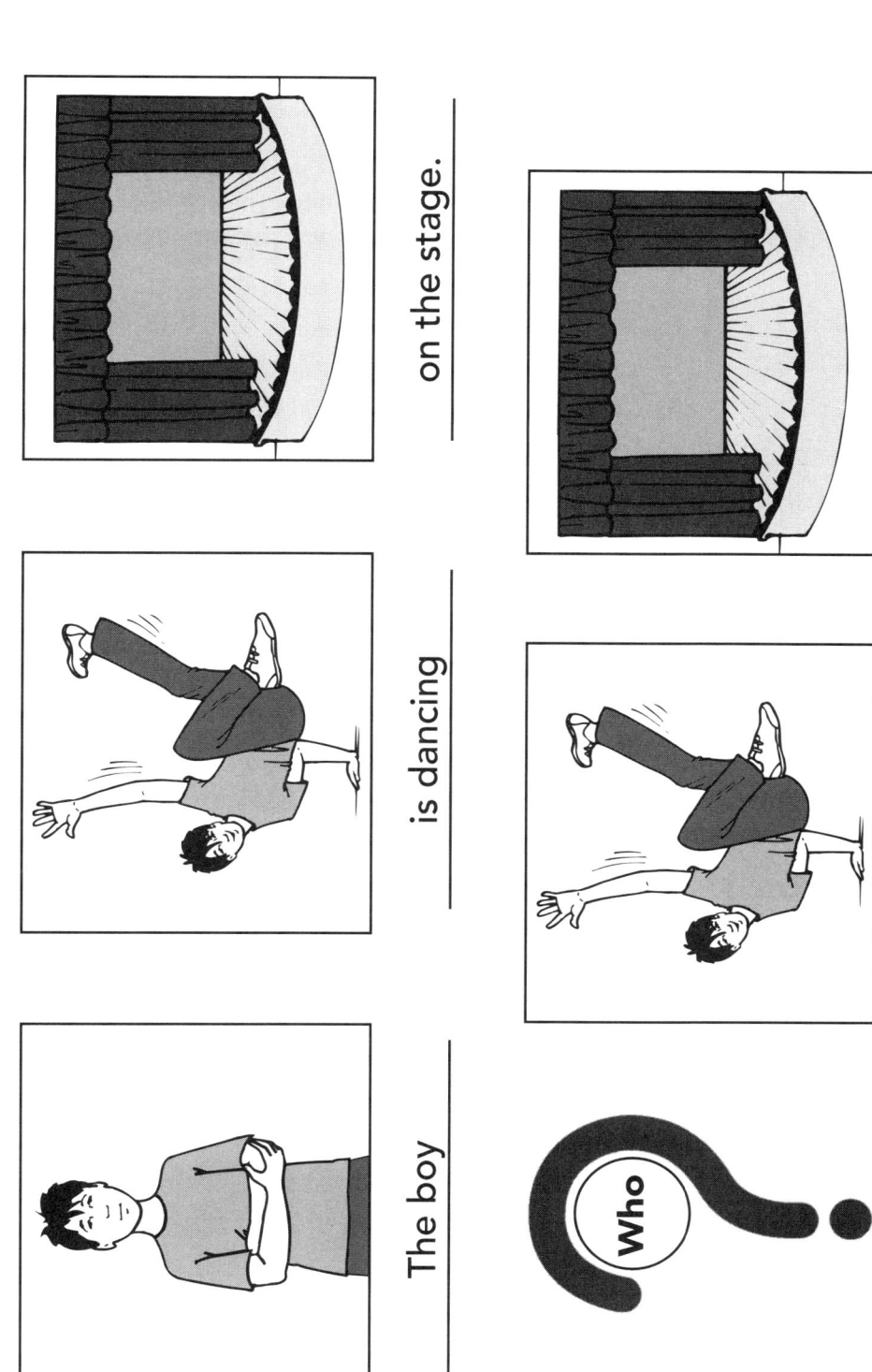

The boy ___ is dancing ___ on the stage.

Who?

The runners will rest on the grass.

Who?

  will march 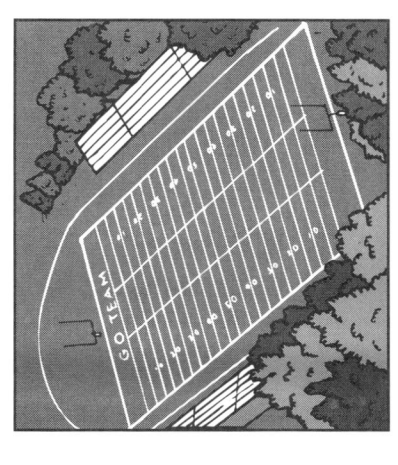 on the field.

 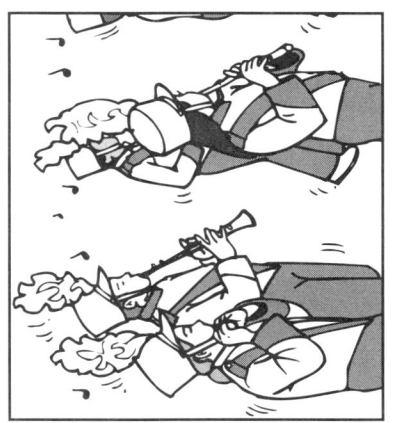 

Unit Review

Write a question that starts with **who** for each picture.

_____?

_____

_____

_____

_____

Unit Review, continued

Write a question that starts with **who** for each picture.

_____

_____

_____

_____

_____

Unit Review, continued

Write a question that starts with **who** for each picture.

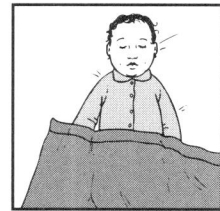

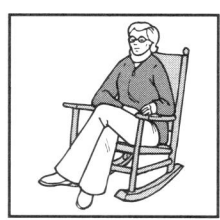

Unit Review, continued

Write a question that starts with **who** for each picture.

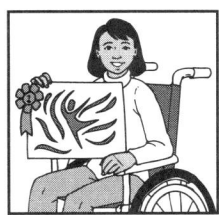

Where Questions

1. Where is the book?
2. Where is the fish?
3. Where is the letter?
4. Where is the bike?
5. Where is the tractor?
6. Where is the ribbon?
7. Where is the Statue of Liberty?
8. Where is the football field?
9. Where is the eagle's nest?
10. Where are the boys?
11. Where are the girls?
12. Where are the apples?
13. Where are the cups?
14. Where are his sunglasses?
15. Where are the puppies sleeping?
16. Where do I get gas?
17. Where do we check out books?
18. Where does the girl put the shirt?
19. Where should we put our boots?
20. Where should we park our car?

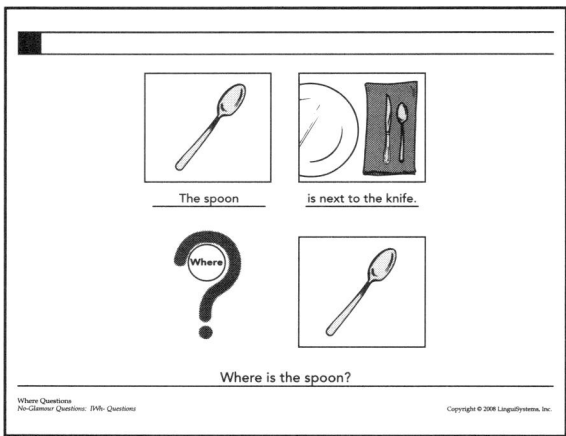

Modeling Script:

1. Look at the pictures at the top of the page. Let's point to the pictures and tell what is happening. **The spoon is next to the knife.**

2. Now look at the pictures at the bottom of the page. When you see this big question mark, you start with the question word inside the circle. This word is **where.**

3. Now let's ask the whole question while we point to each picture. **Where is the spoon?**

4. Now let's write the words under each picture. Remember, a written question ends with a question mark.

1

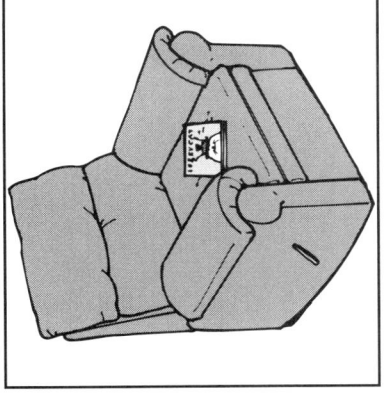

The book _____

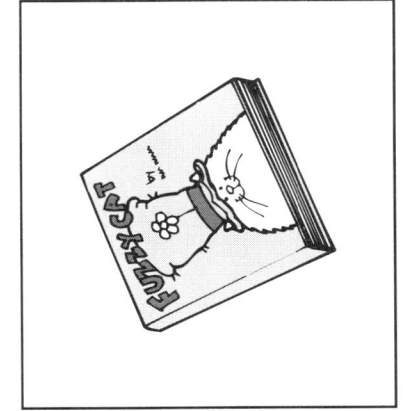

_____ is on the chair.

Where?

2

The fish

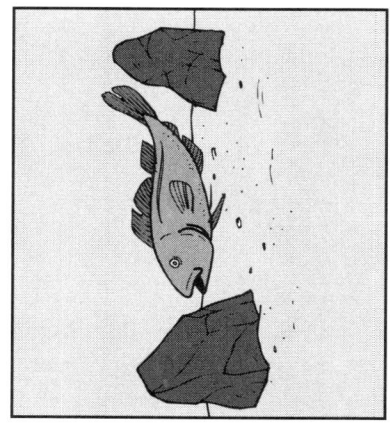

is between the rocks.

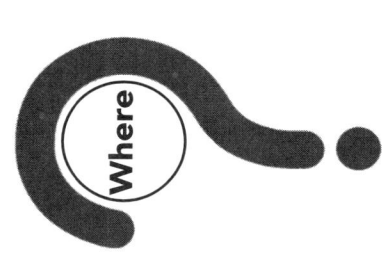

Where?

3

The letter 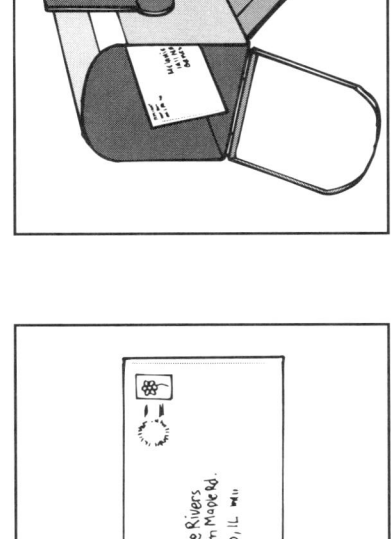 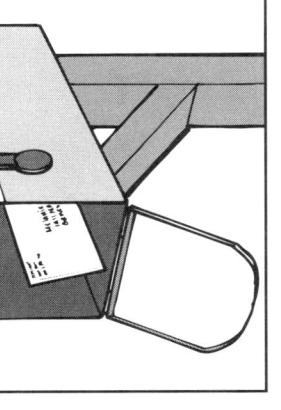 is in the mailbox.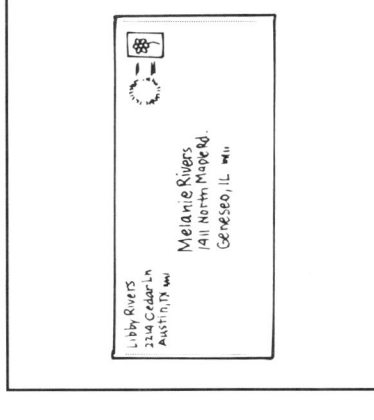

 Where?

Where Questions

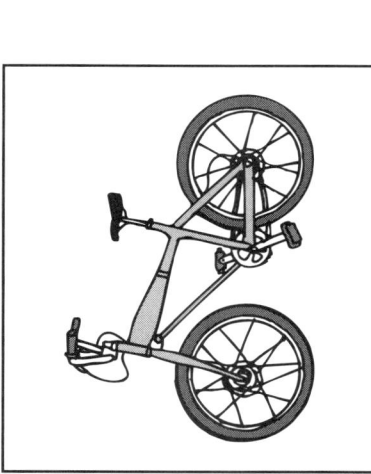

The bike  is next to the tree.

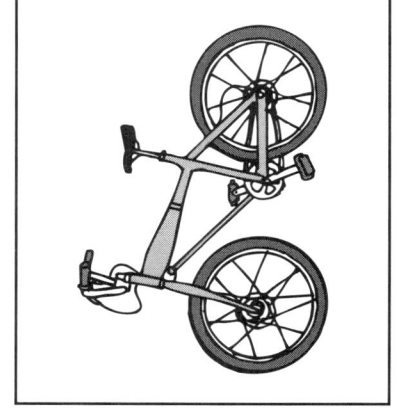

The tractor _____ is near the barn.

Where?

Where Questions
No-Glamour Question Structure: Wh- Questions

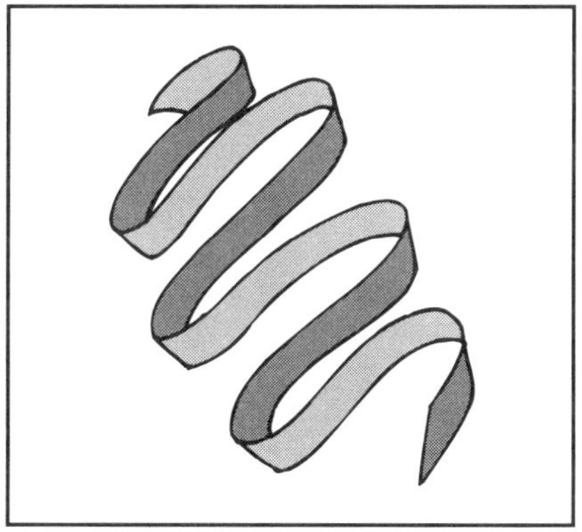

The ribbon _____ is around the present. _____

Where?

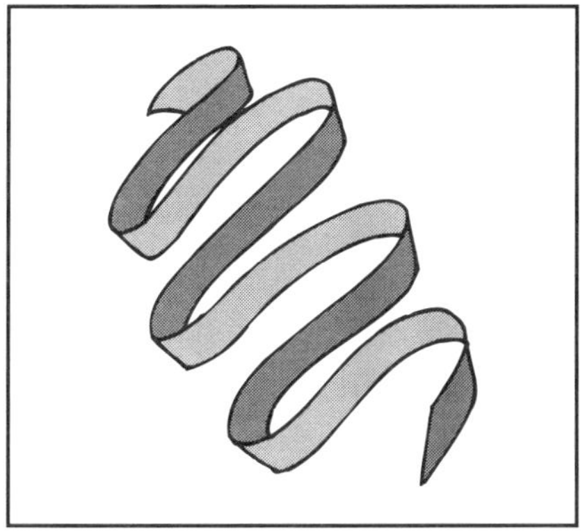

7

The Statue of Liberty _____ is in New York.

Where?

Where Questions
No-Glamour Question Structure: Wh- Questions

Copyright © 2008 LinguiSystems, Inc.

8

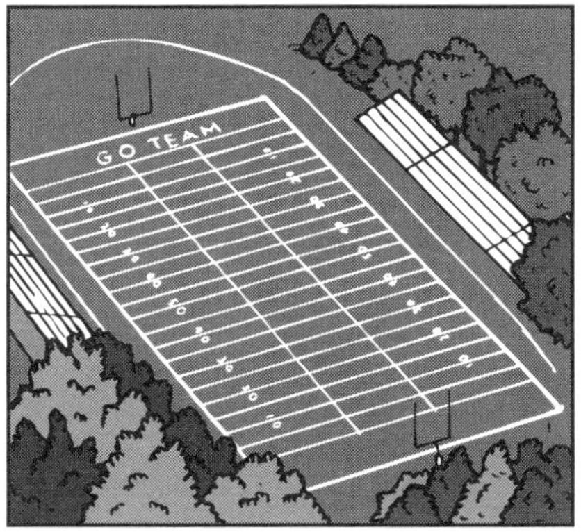

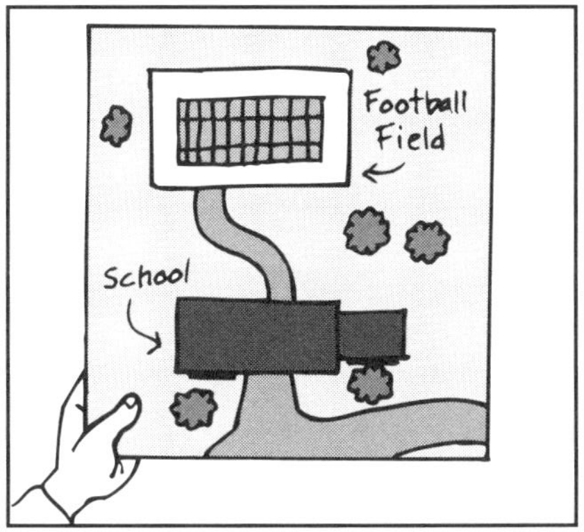

The football field _____ is behind the school.

Where?

The eagle's nest _____ is in the oak tree.

Where?

10

The boys _____ are under the table.

Where?

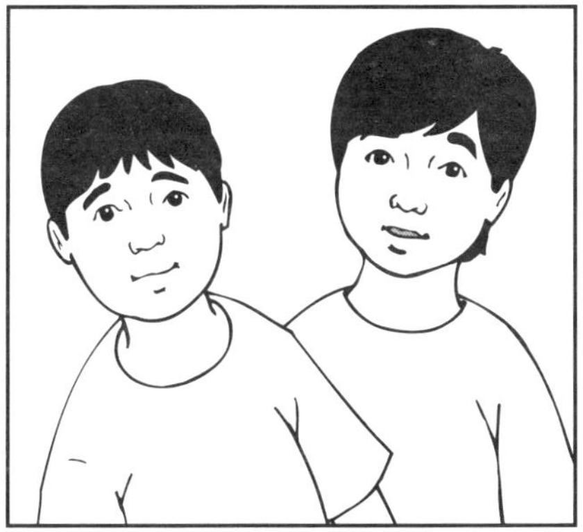

11

The girls _____ are in front of Sam.

Where?

12

The apples _____ are in the bowl.

Where?

Where Questions
No-Glamour Question Structure: Wh- Questions

13

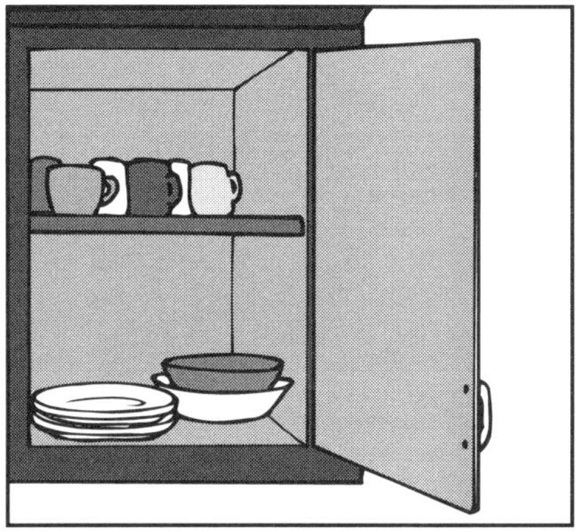

The cups _____ are on the top shelf.

Where?

Where Questions
No-Glamour Question Structure: Wh- Questions

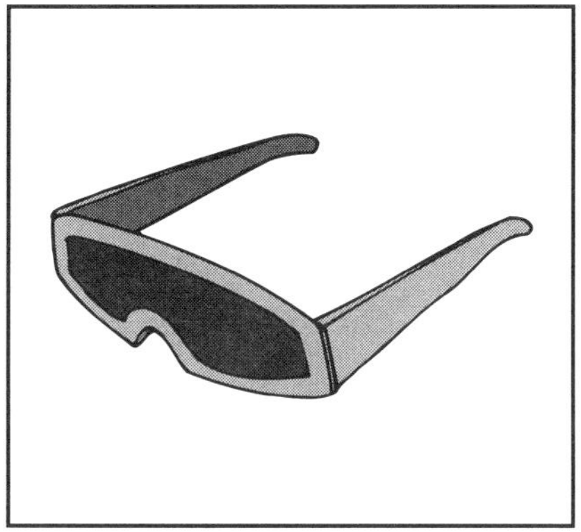

14

His sunglasses _____ are on his head.

Where?

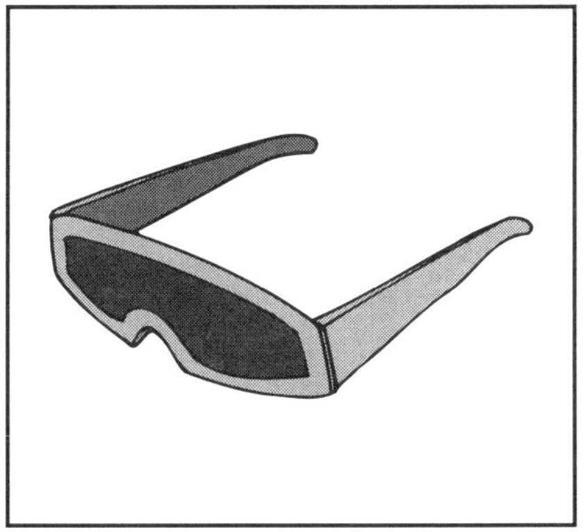

15

The puppies _____ are sleeping _____ beside their mother.

Where?

Where Questions
No-Glamour Question Structure: Wh- Questions

16

Where do I _____ get gas _____ at the gas station.

Where Questions
No-Glamour Question Structure: Wh- Questions

17

check out books

at the library.

We

Where do ?

Where Questions
No-Glamour Question Structure: Wh- Questions

Copyright © 2008 LinguiSystems, Inc.

49

The girl puts the shirt in the drawer.

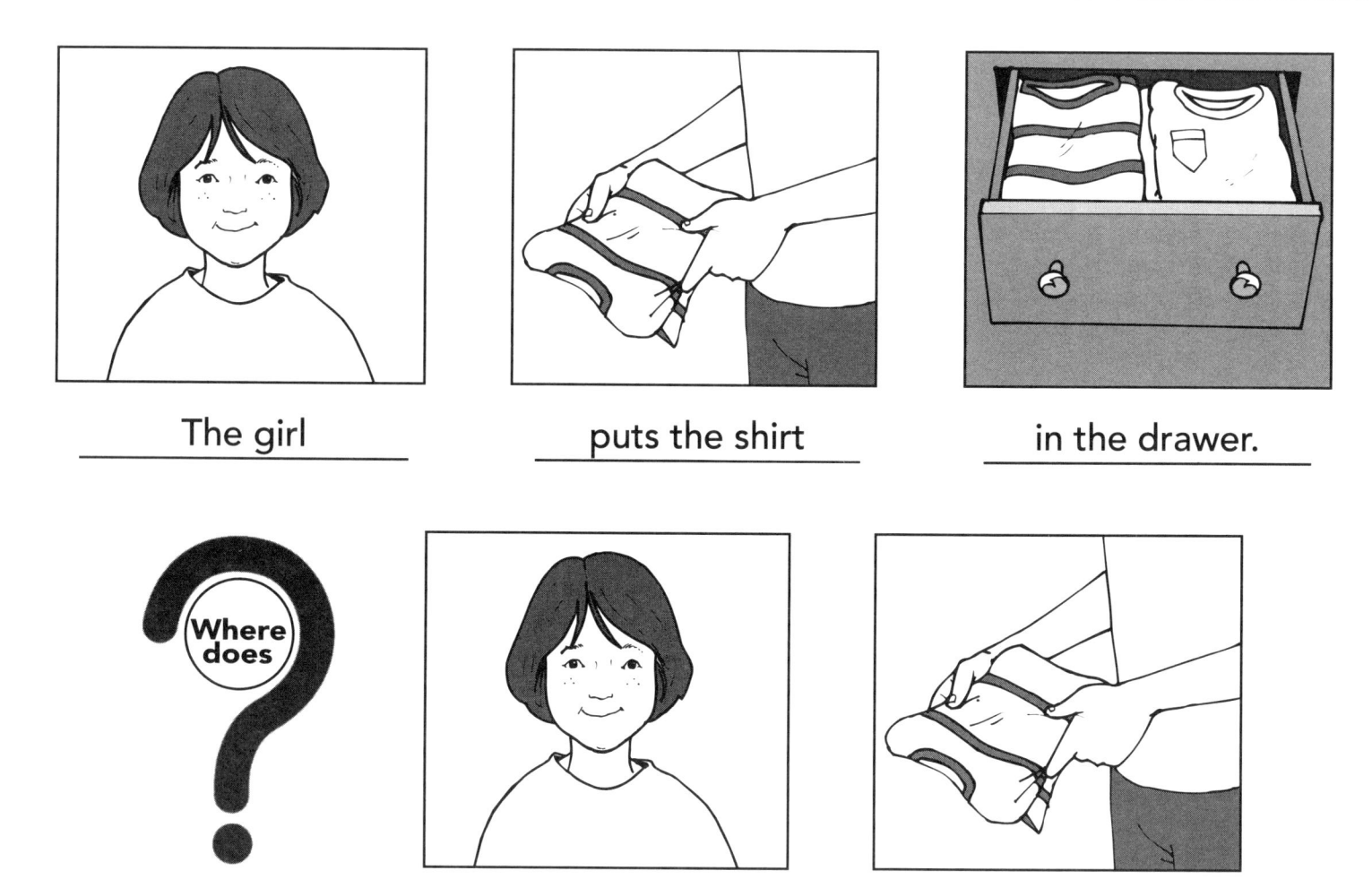

Where does ?

19

We 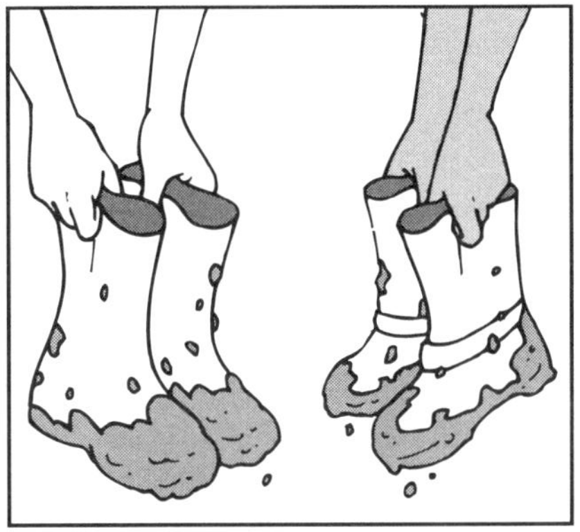 _____ should put our boots  _____ outside the door.

Where?

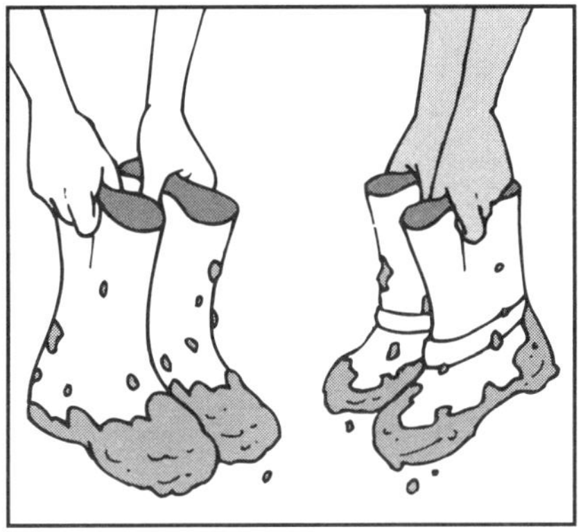

Where Questions

20

We _____ should park our car _____ in the driveway.

Where ?

Where Questions
No-Glamour Question Structure: Wh- Questions

Unit Review

Write a question that starts with **where** for each picture.

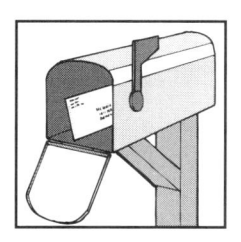

_____?

_____

_____

_____

_____

Unit Review, continued

Write a question that starts with **where** for each picture.

Unit Review, continued

Write a question that starts with **where** for each picture.

Where Questions
No-Glamour Question Structure: Wh- Questions

Unit Review, continued

Write a question that starts with **where** for each picture.

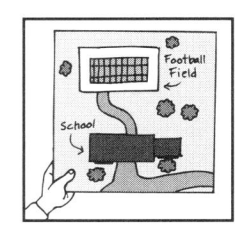

Where Questions
No-Glamour Question Structure: Wh- Questions

When Questions

1. When do I close my eyes?
2. When do we eat lunch?
3. When do you play outside?
4. When do you use a Band-Aid?
5. When do we wear pajamas?
6. When do I open the window?
7. When do I wear a coat?
8. When do new leaves grow on trees?
9. When does Anna wear a seatbelt?
10. When does the girl dance?
11. When does Sarah wear glasses?
12. When does a dog bark?
13. When can you see the moon?
14. When can you see a rainbow?
15. When can we have bare feet?
16. When will the audience clap?
17. When will the chick hatch?
18. When will the sun rise?
19. When will the player shout "hooray"?
20. When should I stay in bed?

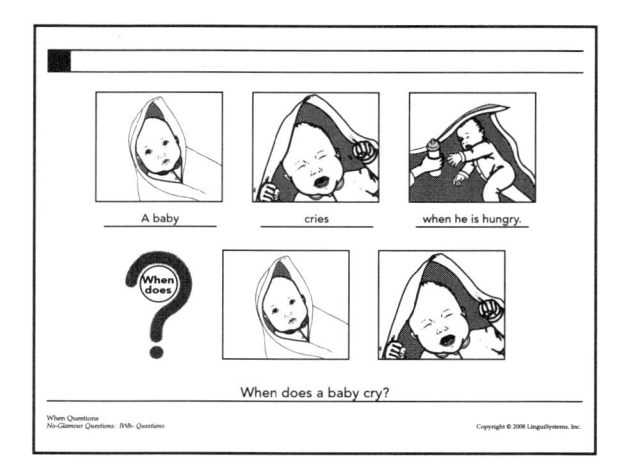

Modeling Script:

1. Look at the pictures at the top of the page. Let's point to the pictures and tell what is happening. **A baby cries when he is hungry.**
2. Now look at the pictures at the bottom of the page. When you see this big question mark, you start with the question word inside the circle. This word is **when**.
3. Now let's ask the whole question while we point to each picture. **When does a baby cry?**
4. Now let's write the words under each picture. Remember, a written question ends with a question mark.

1

I  _____ close my eyes  _____ when I make a wish.

When do _____?

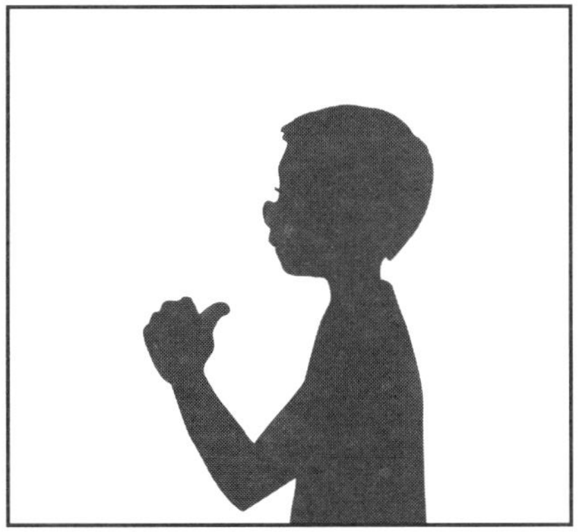

When Questions
No-Glamour Question Structure: Wh- Questions

Copyright © 2008 LinguiSystems, Inc.

When do _____ **We** _____ **eat lunch** _____ **at noon.**

3

You | play outside | on a sunny day.

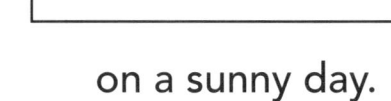

When do ?

When Questions
No-Glamour Question Structure: Wh- Questions

4

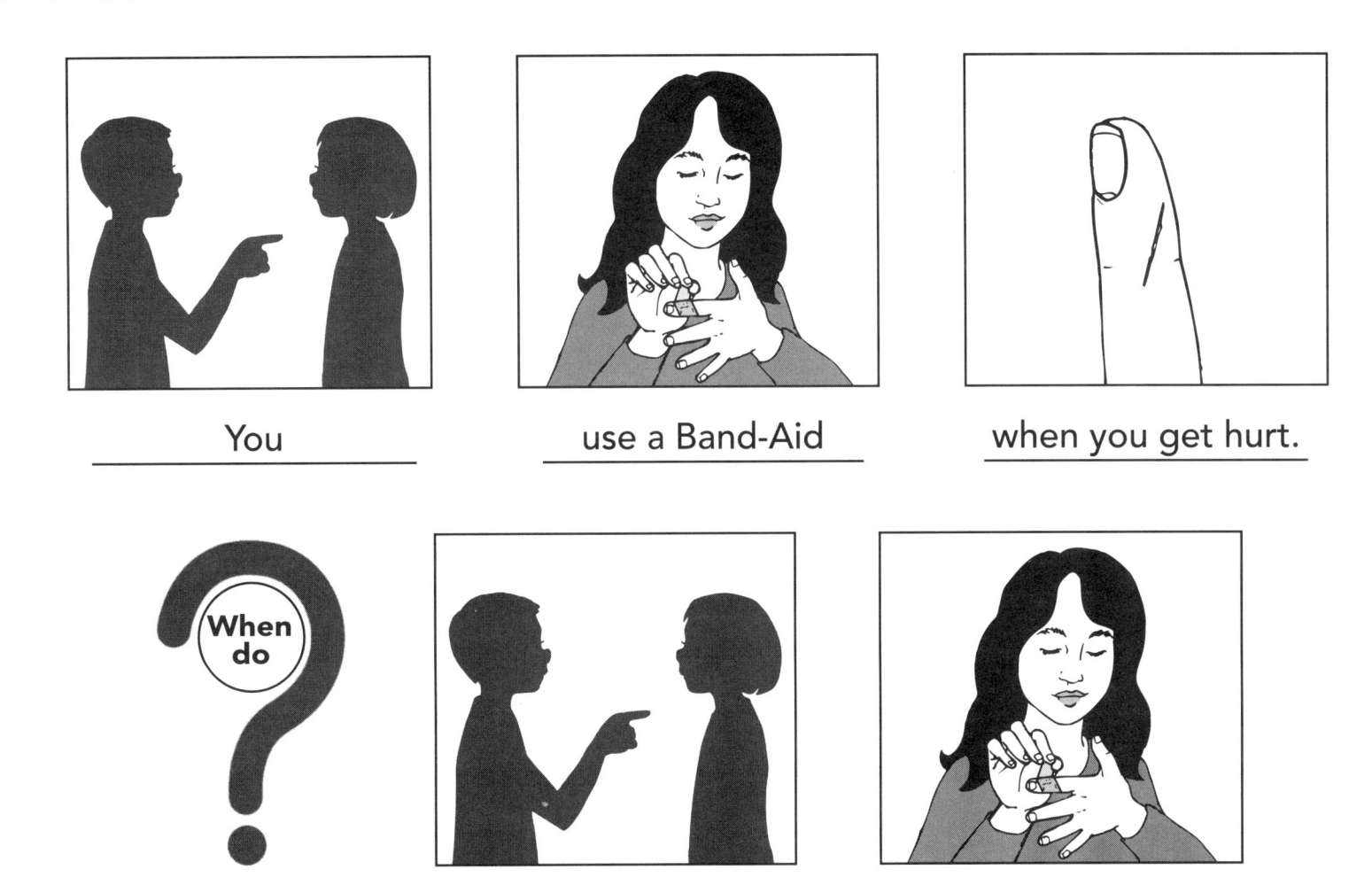

When do

You   use a Band-Aid   when you get hurt.

When Questions
No-Glamour Question Structure: Wh- Questions

Copyright © 2008 LinguiSystems, Inc.

61

5

wear pajamas — when we go to bed.

We —

When do ?

When Questions
No-Glamour Question Structure: Wh- Questions

When Questions

When do ?

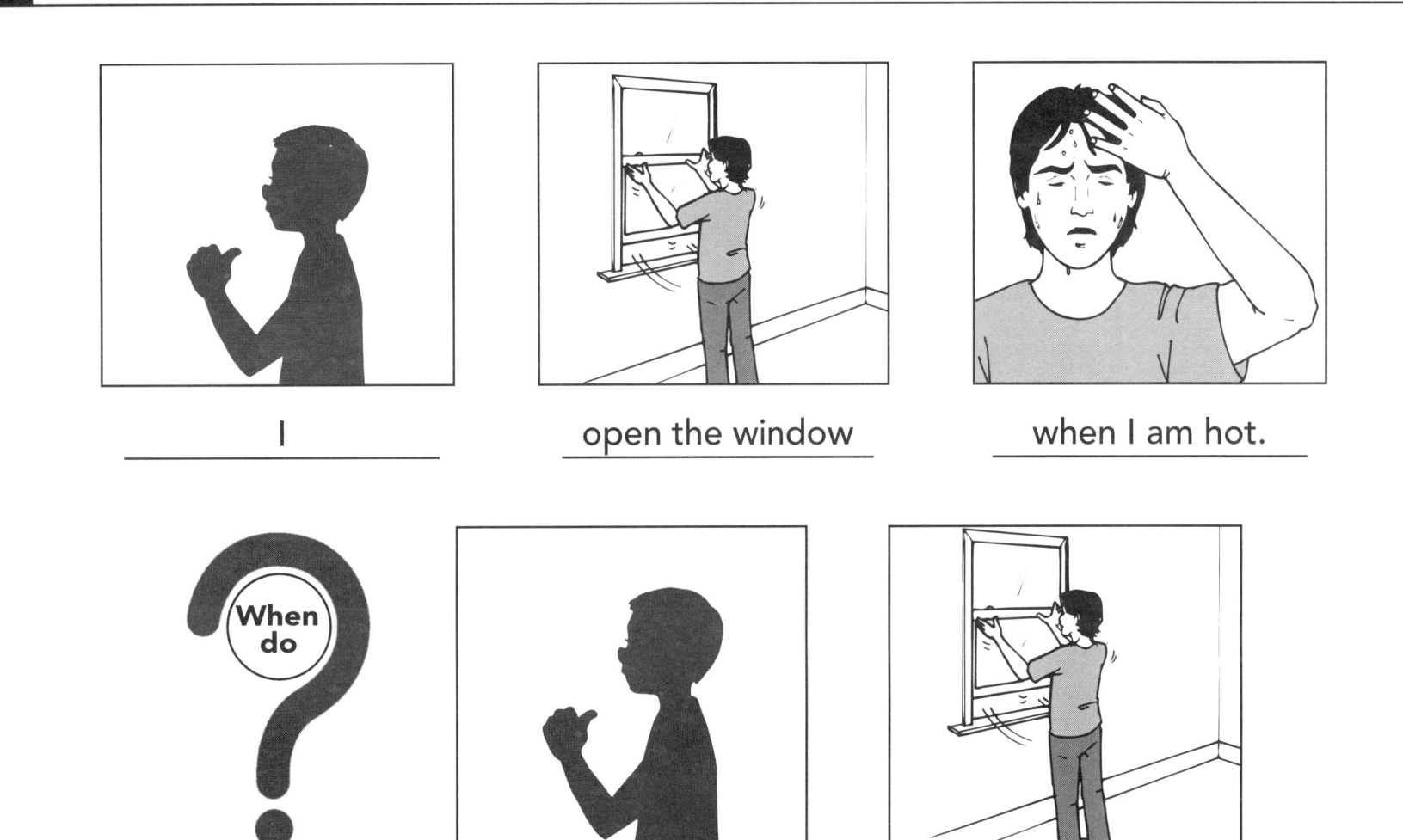

I _____ open the window _____ when I am hot.

7

I _____ wear a coat _____ when I am cold.

When do _____?

When Questions
No-Glamour Question Structure: Wh- Questions

New leaves _____ grow on trees _____ in the spring.

When do

9

Anna wears a seatbelt when she is in a car.

When does ?

10

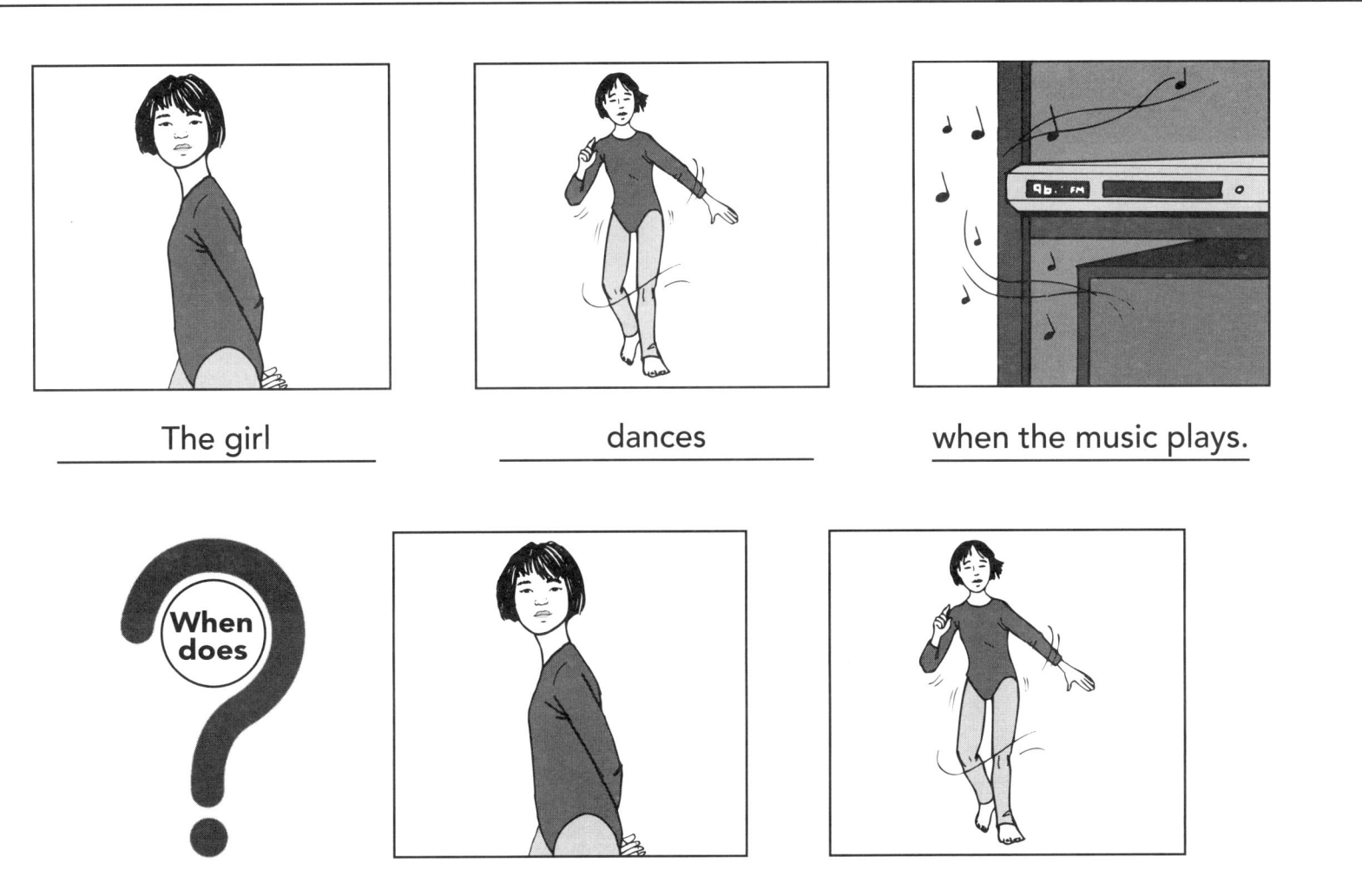

The girl _____ dances _____ when the music plays.

When does ?

When Questions
No-Glamour Question Structure: Wh- Questions

11

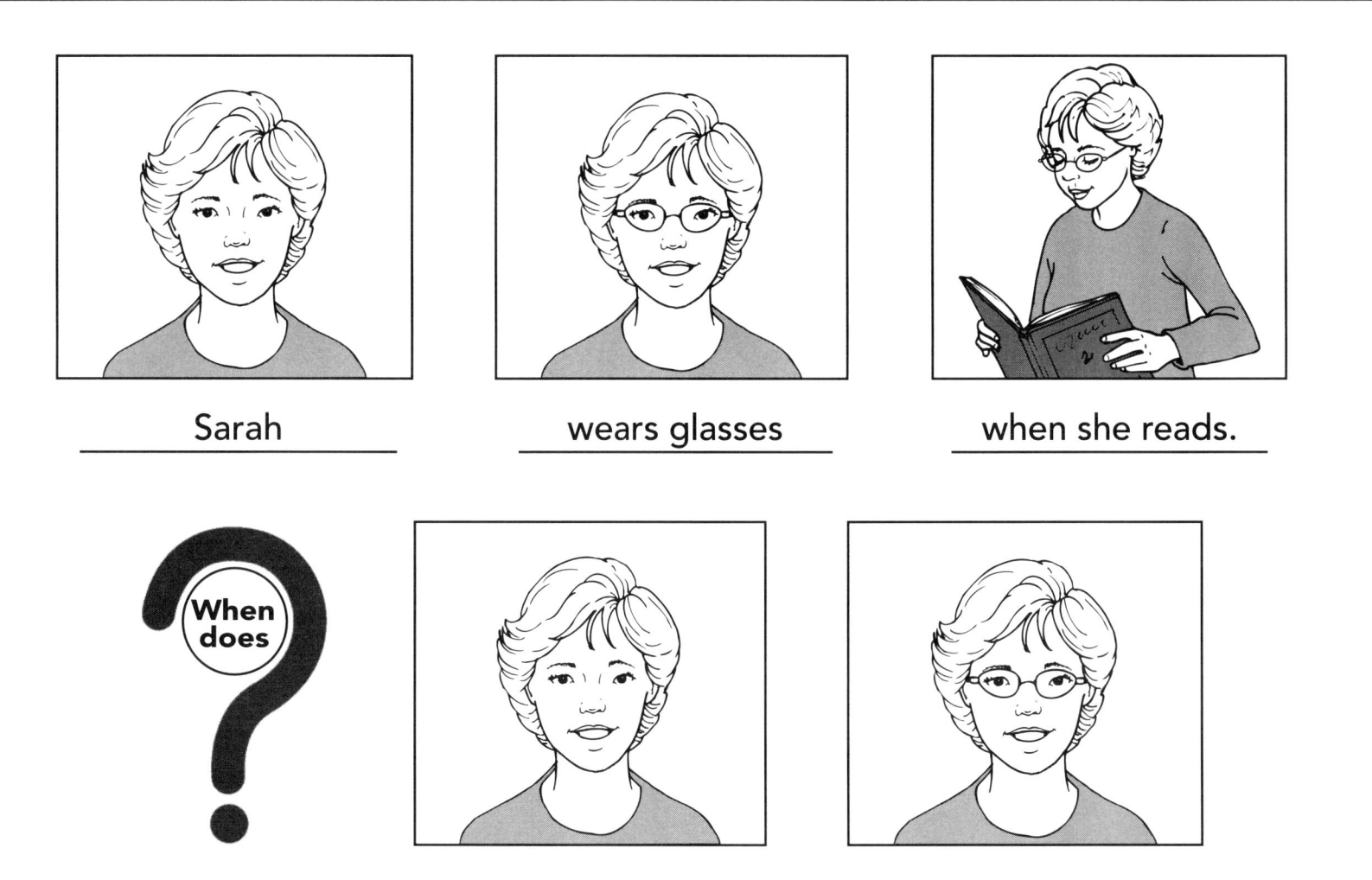

Sarah | wears glasses | when she reads.

When does

When Questions
No-Glamour Question Structure: Wh- Questions

12

A dog | barks | when it sees a cat.

When does ?

When Questions
No-Glamour Question Structure: Wh- Questions

13

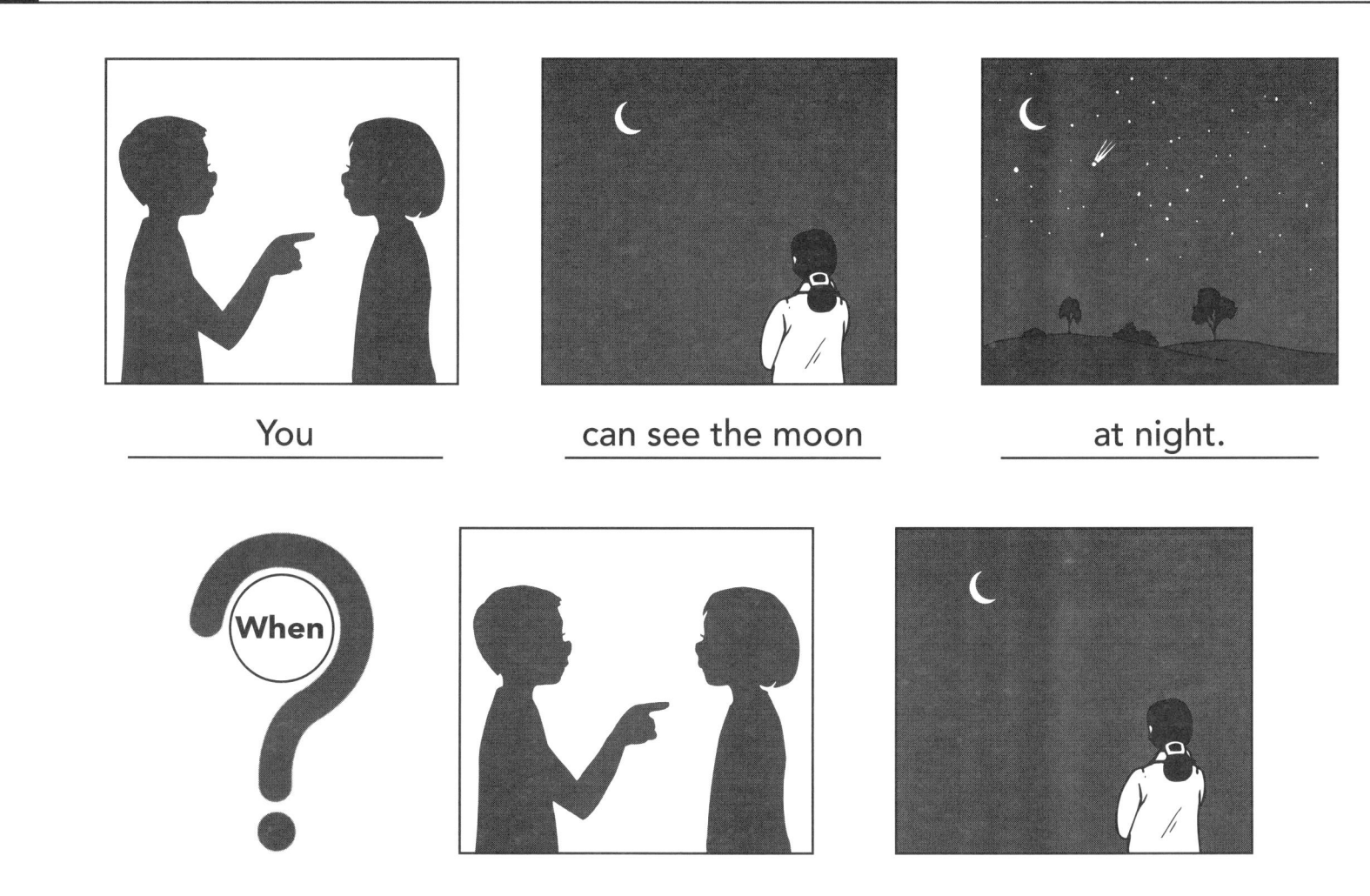

You _____ can see the moon _____ at night.

When?

14

You _____ can see a rainbow _____ after it rains.

When?

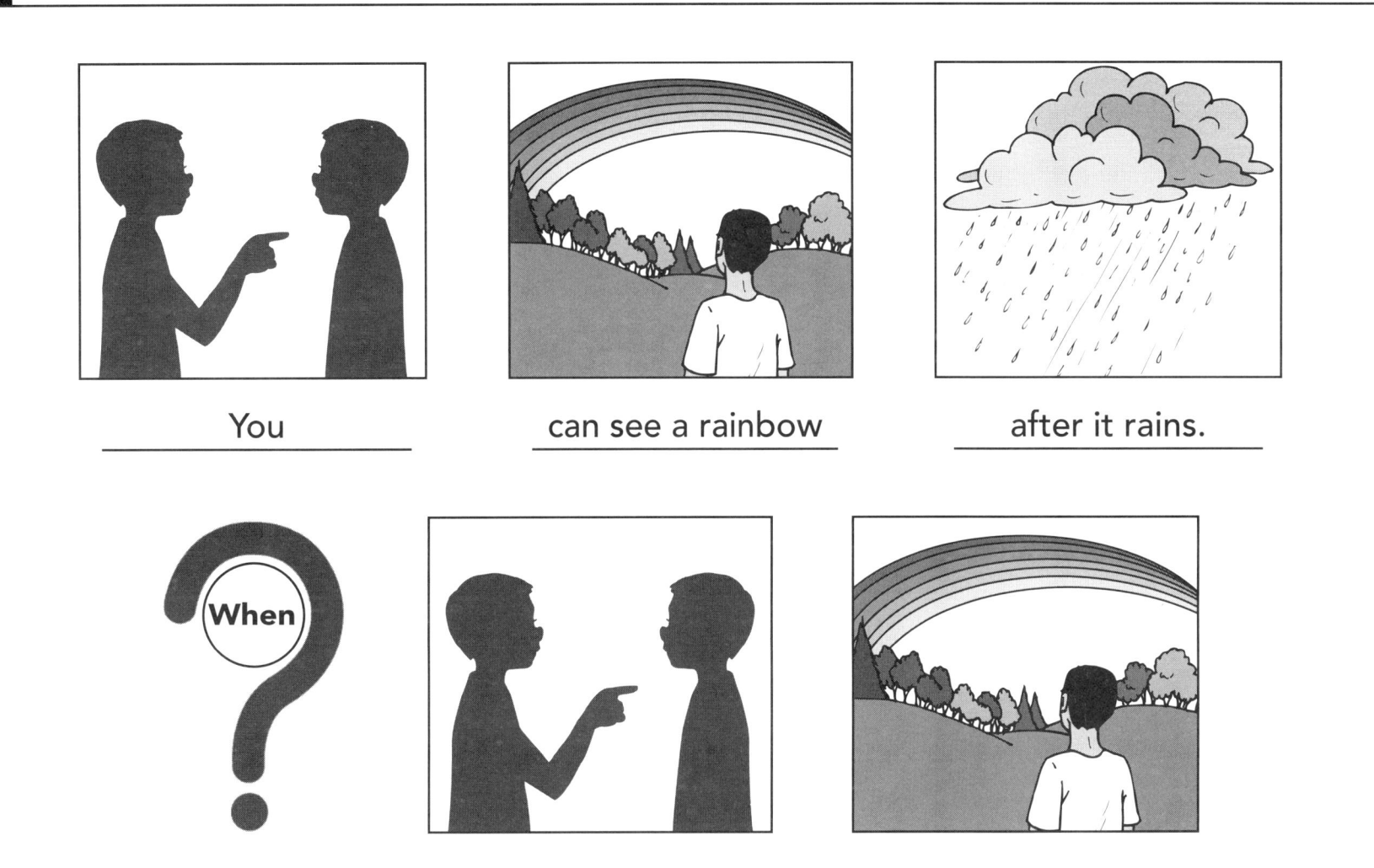

When Questions
No-Glamour Question Structure: Wh- Questions

71

15

We 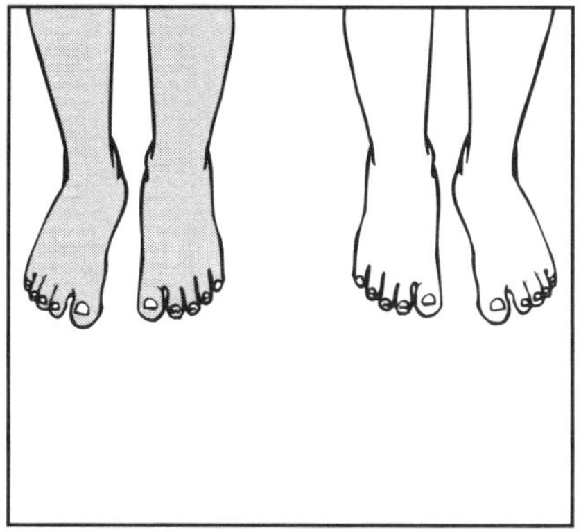 ____ can have bare feet  ____ when we swim.

When ?

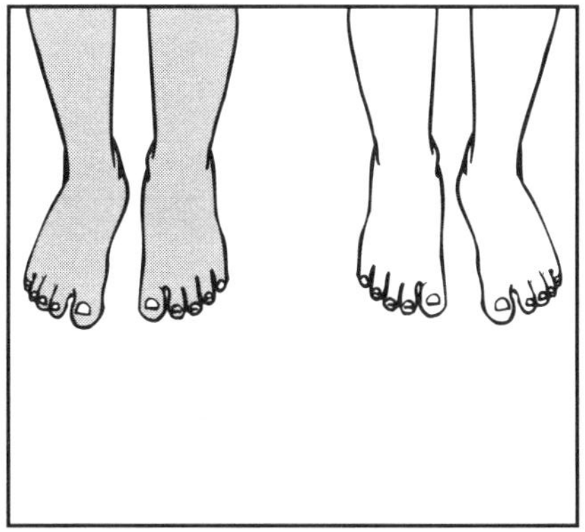

When Questions
No-Glamour Question Structure: Wh- Questions

16

The audience　　will clap　　when the play ends.

When?

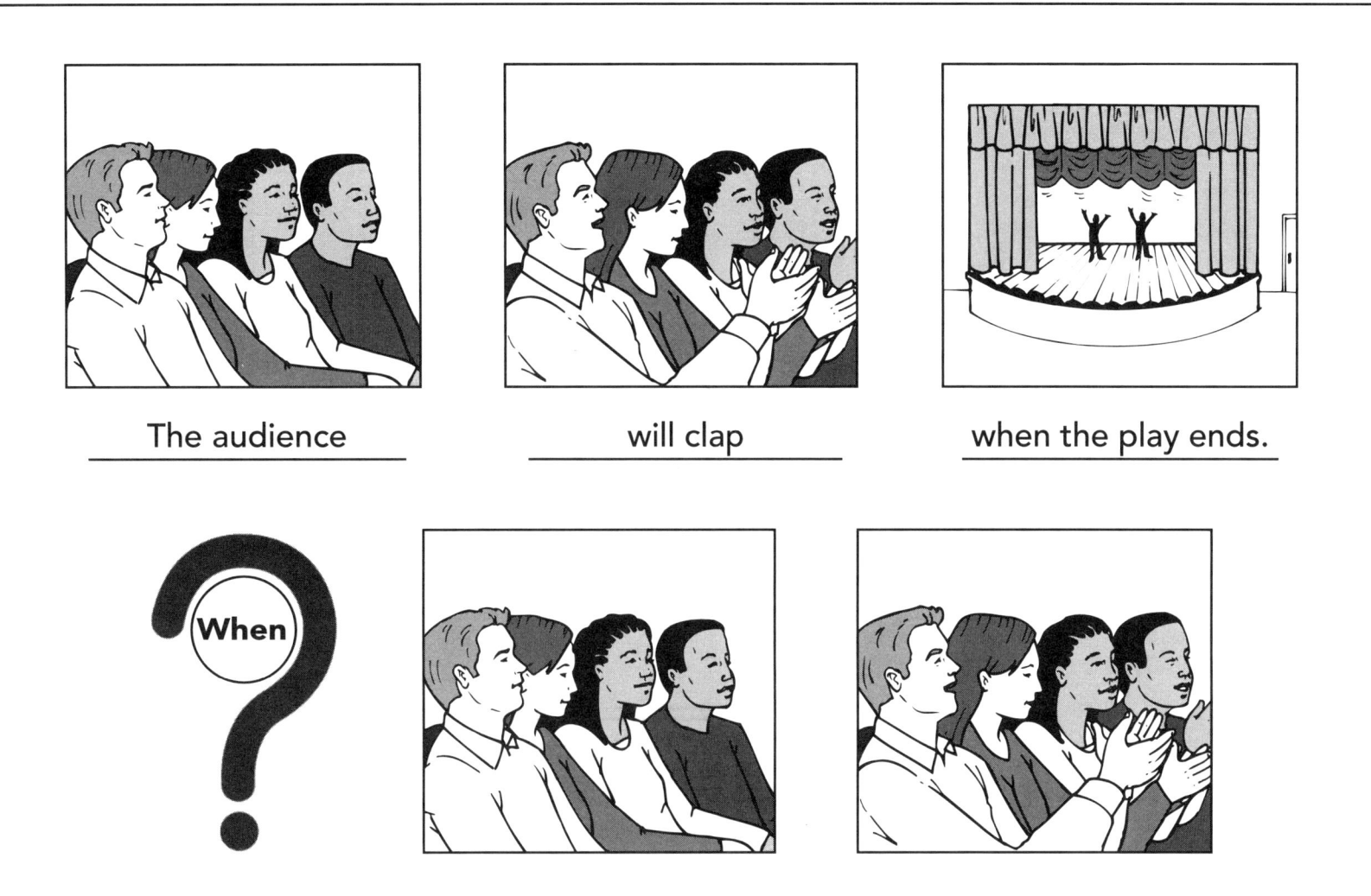

When Questions
No-Glamour Question Structure: Wh- Questions

17

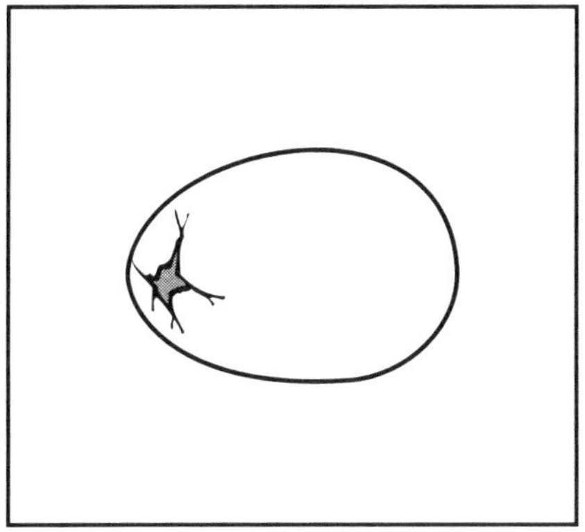

The chick _____ will hatch _____ when the egg cracks.

When?

When Questions
No-Glamour Question Structure: Wh- Questions

18

The sun | will rise | at 6 a.m.

When?

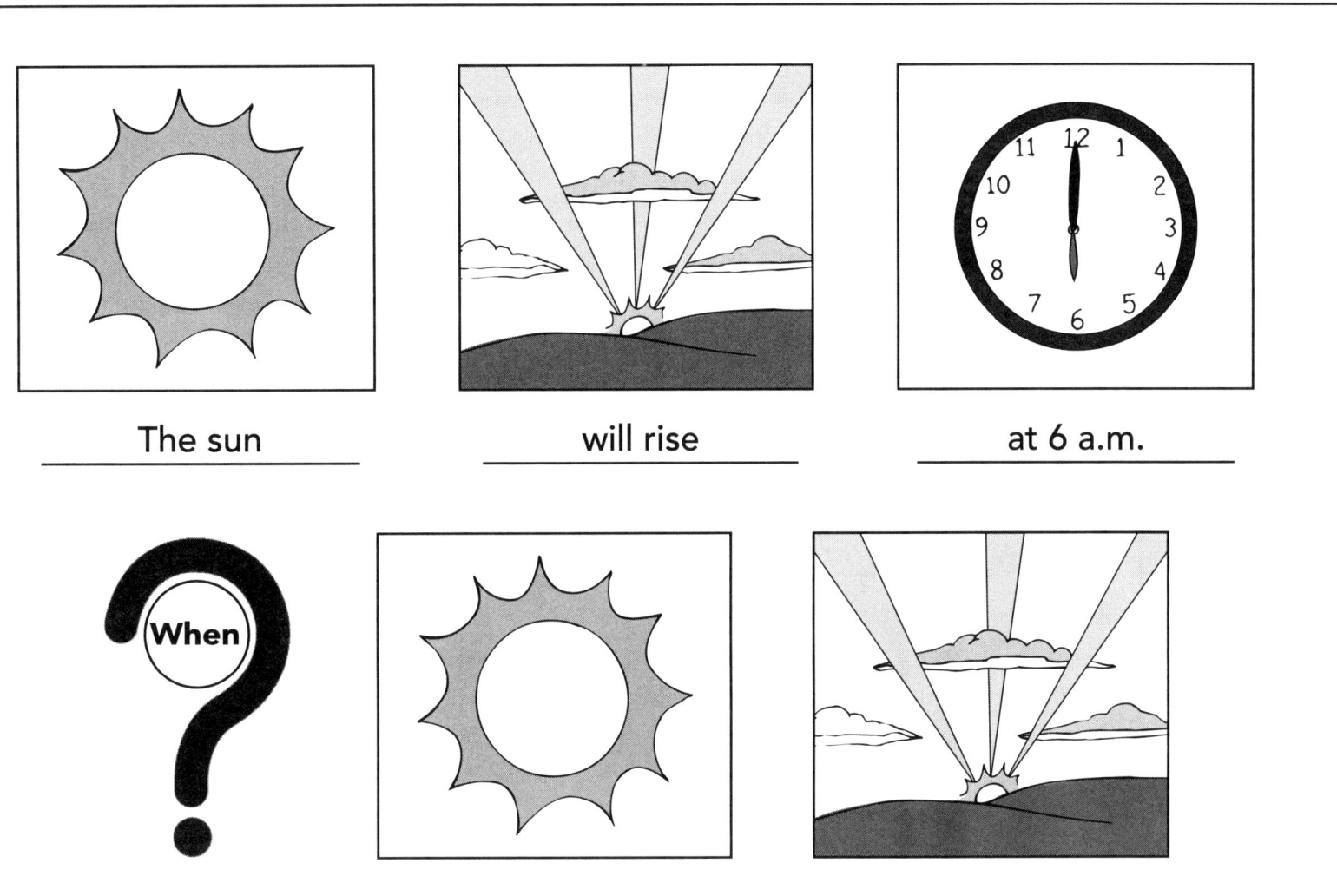

When Questions
No-Glamour Question Structure: Wh- Questions

19

The player will shout "hooray" after he scores.

When?

20

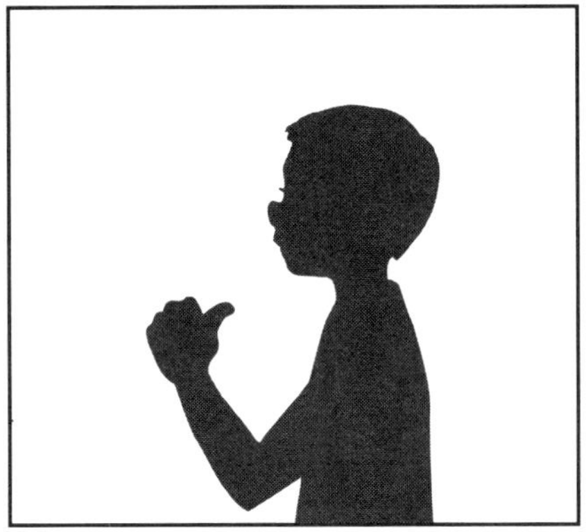

I _____ should stay in bed _____ when I am sick.

When _____ ?

Unit Review

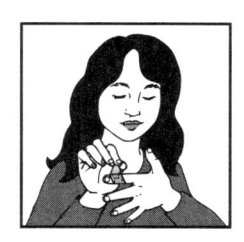

Write a question that starts with **when** for each picture.

_____?

_____

_____

_____

_____

When Questions
No-Glamour Question Structure: Wh- Questions

Unit Review, continued

Write a question that starts with **when** for each picture.

Unit Review, continued

Write a question that starts with **when** for each picture.

When Questions
No-Glamour Question Structure: Wh- Questions

Unit Review, continued

Write a question that starts with **when** for each picture.

When Questions
No-Glamour Question Structure: Wh- Questions

What Questions

1. What is in the box?
2. What is on the shelf?
3. What is under the bed?
4. What is in her purse?
5. What floats away?
6. What tells time?
7. What holds up my pants?
8. What cleans my hands?
9. What comes after Friday?
10. What comes before math?
11. What tastes good on popcorn?
12. What is Lily riding?
13. What is the worker opening?
14. What are we eating?
15. What happens if a wave hits a sand castle?
16. What happens if you pet a cat?
17. What happens if you water flowers?
18. What does Grandpa use to gather leaves?
19. What does the girl use to cut yarn?
20. What does Jack put on to play in the snow?

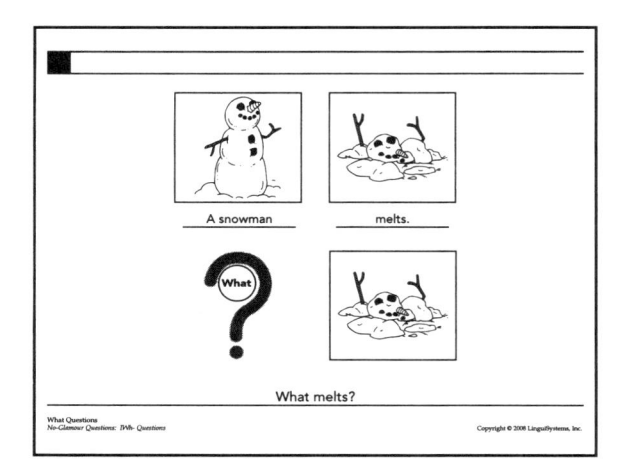

Modeling Script:

1. Look at the pictures at the top of the page. Let's point to the pictures and tell what is happening. **A snowman melts.**

2. Now look at the pictures at the bottom of the page. When you see this big question mark, you start with the question word inside the circle. This word is **what**.

3. Now let's ask the whole question while we point to each picture. **What melts?**

4. Now let's write the words under each picture. Remember, a written question ends with a question mark.

1

A cat _____ is in the box.

What?

2

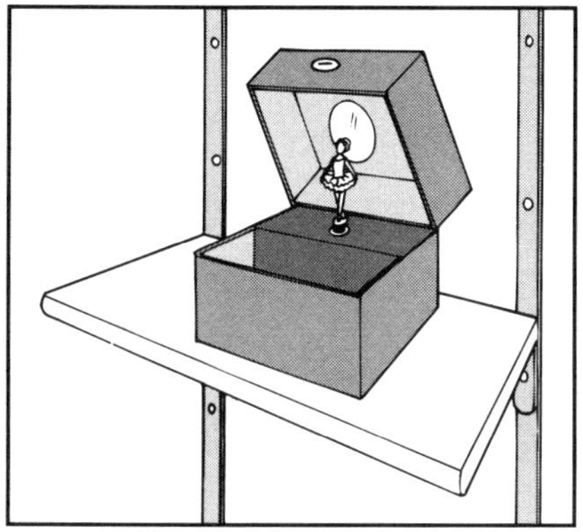

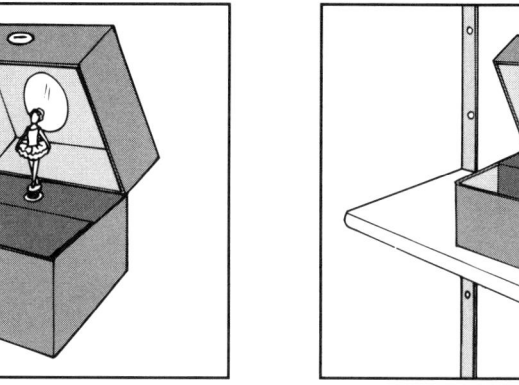

The music box _____ is on the shelf.

What?

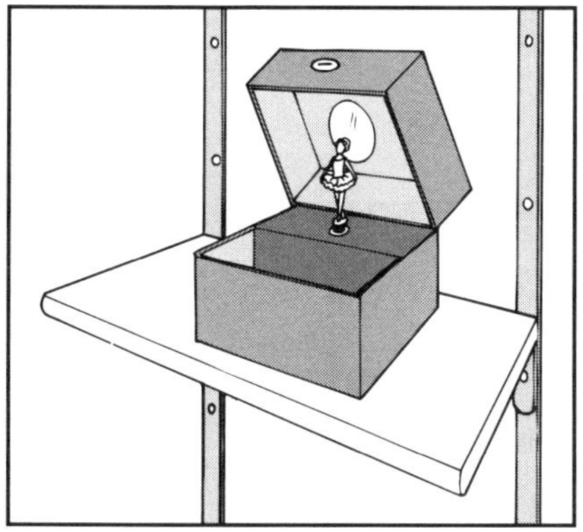

What Questions
No-Glamour Question Structure: Wh- Questions

3

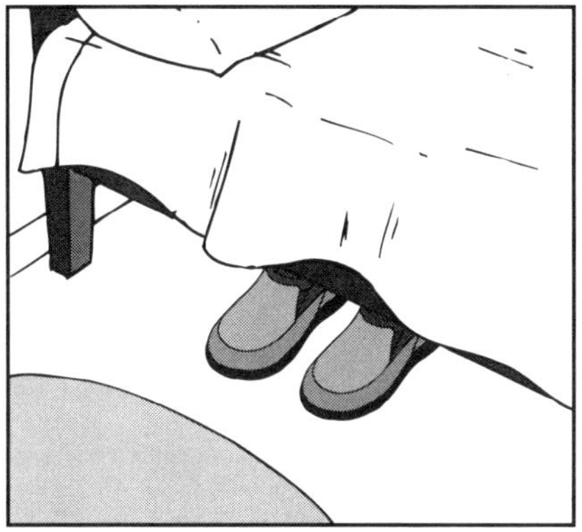

A pair of shoes _____ is under the bed.

What?

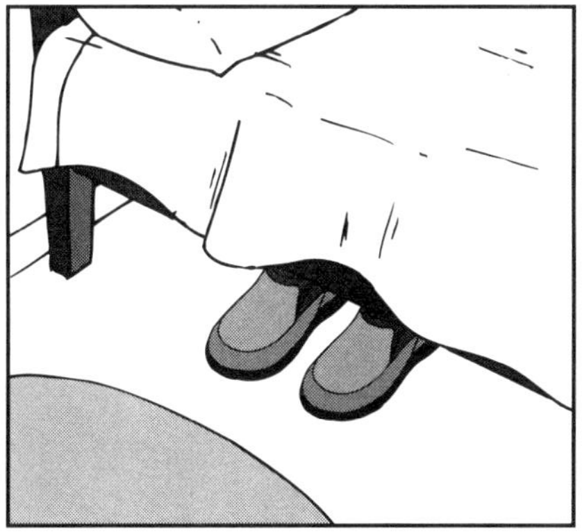

4

The pencil _____ is in her purse.

What?

What Questions
No-Glamour Question Structure: Wh- Questions

5

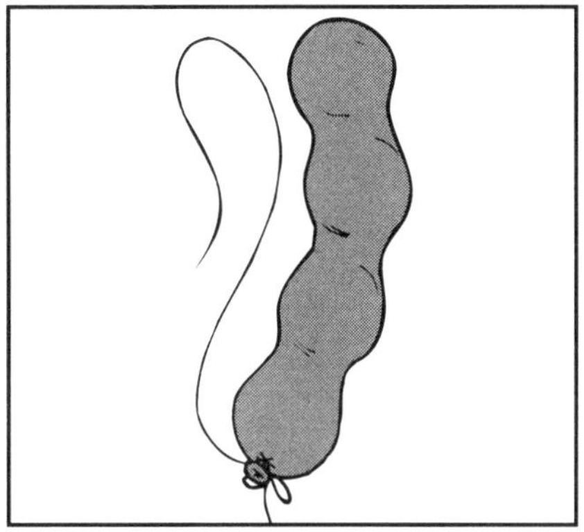

The balloon _____ floats away.

What?

A clock _____ tells time.

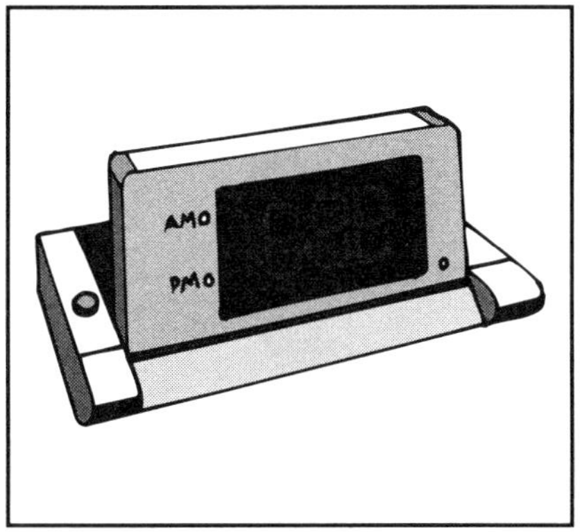

What?

7

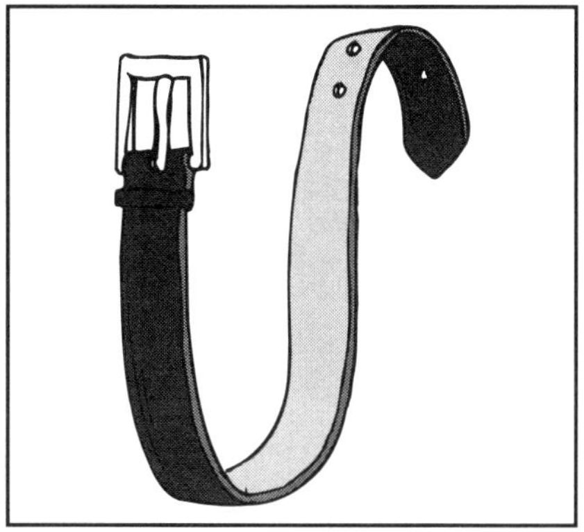

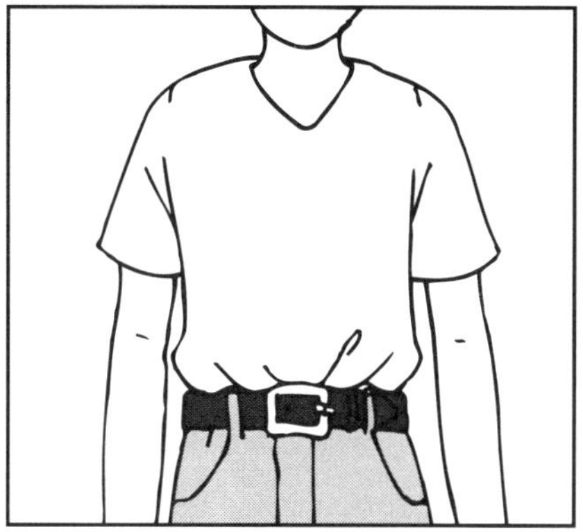

A belt

holds up my pants.

What?

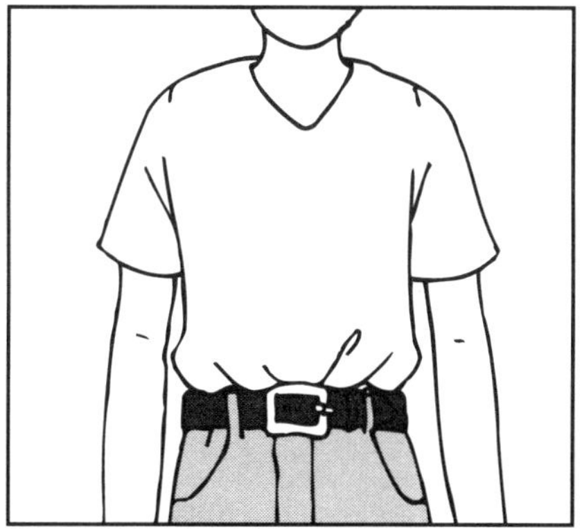

8

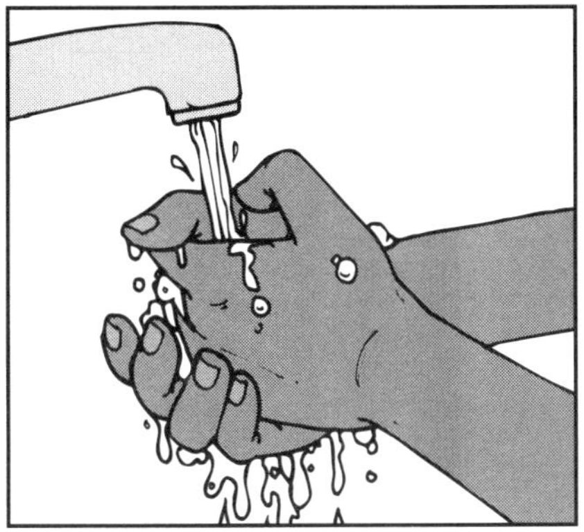

Soap _____ cleans my hands.

What ?

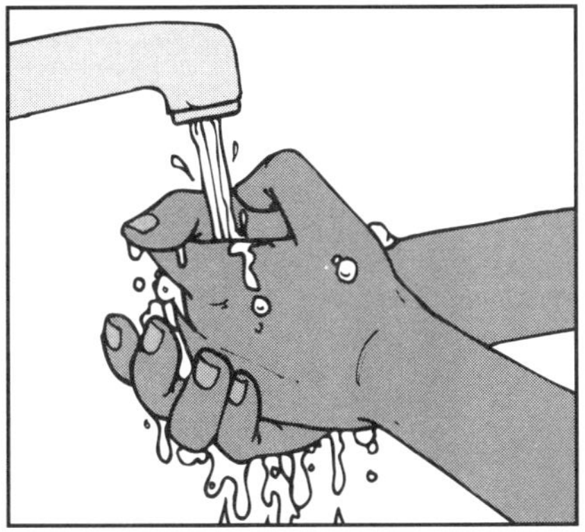

9

Saturday   comes after Friday.

What?

What Questions
No-Glamour Question Structure: Wh- Questions

10

Spelling-9:15	Reading-8:30 Spelling-9:15 Math - 10:00 Lunch - 11:00 Art - 12:00
Spelling	_____ comes before math.

Reading-8:30
Spelling-9:15
Math - 10:00
Lunch - 11:00
Art - 12:00

What?

Salt tastes good on popcorn.

Lily  is riding  a skateboard.

What?

13

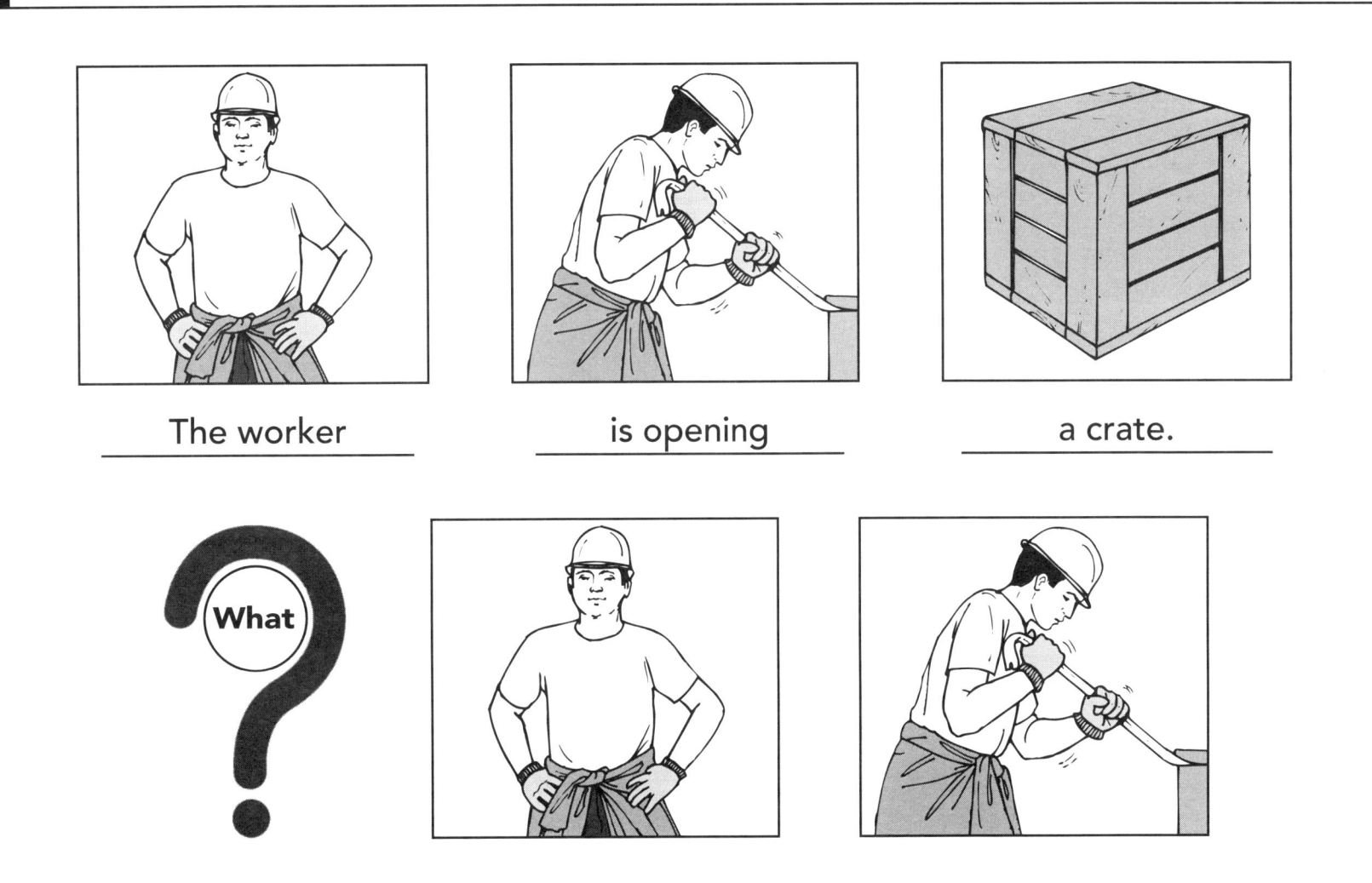

The worker is opening a crate.

What?

14

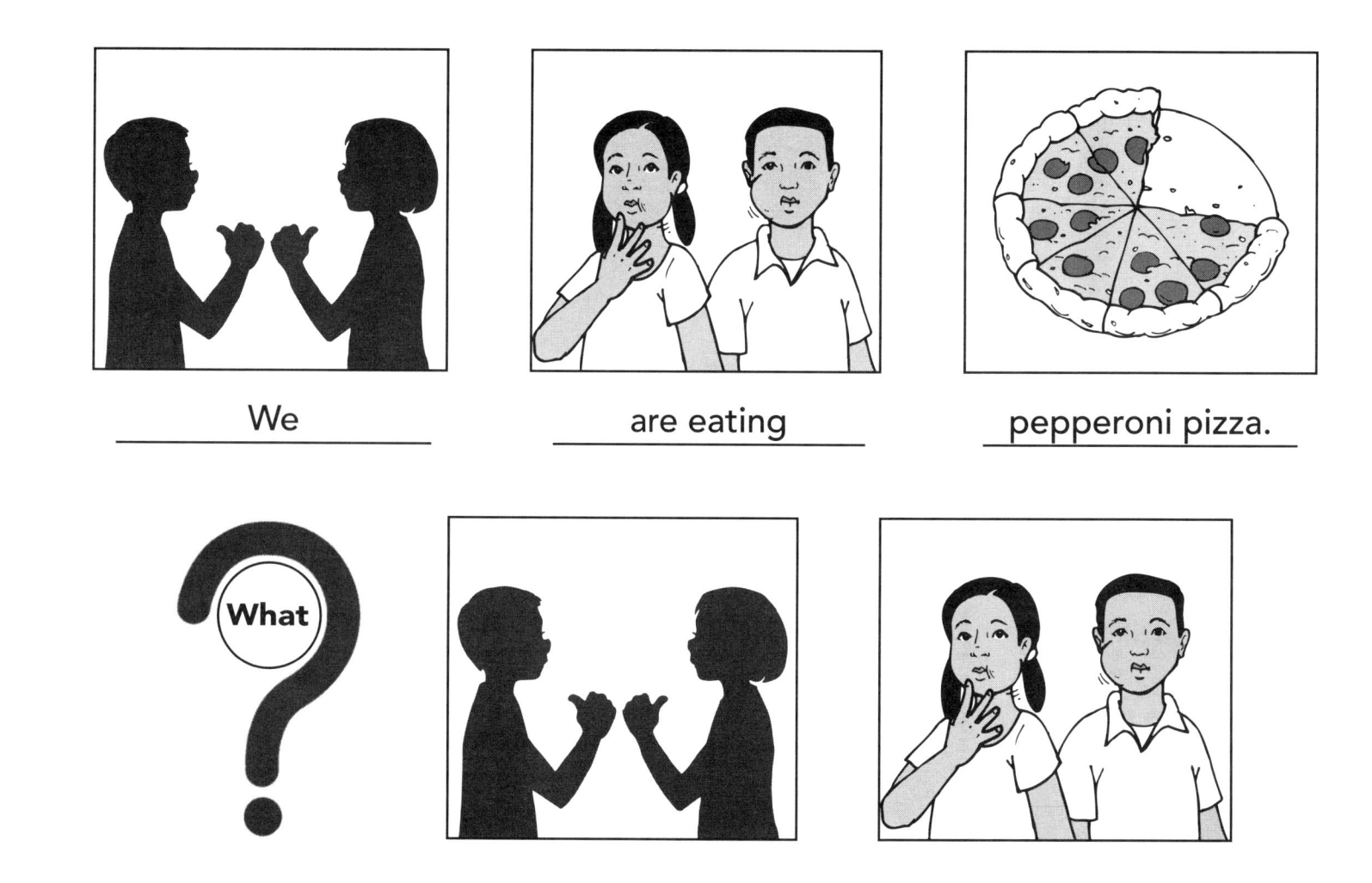

We _____ are eating _____ pepperoni pizza.

What ?

15

If a wave   hits a sand castle,   it will wash away.

What happens?

16

If you  ___ pet a cat,  ___ it will purr.

What happens?

What Questions
No-Glamour Question Structure: Wh- Questions

17

If you  ———— water flowers,  ———— they will grow.

What happens?

18 * The student may need a cue to drop this noun from the question sequence.

Grandpa _____ uses a rake* _____ to gather leaves.

What does

What Questions
No-Glamour Question Structure: Wh- Questions

Copyright © 2008 LinguiSystems, Inc.

19 * The student may need a cue to drop this noun from the question sequence.

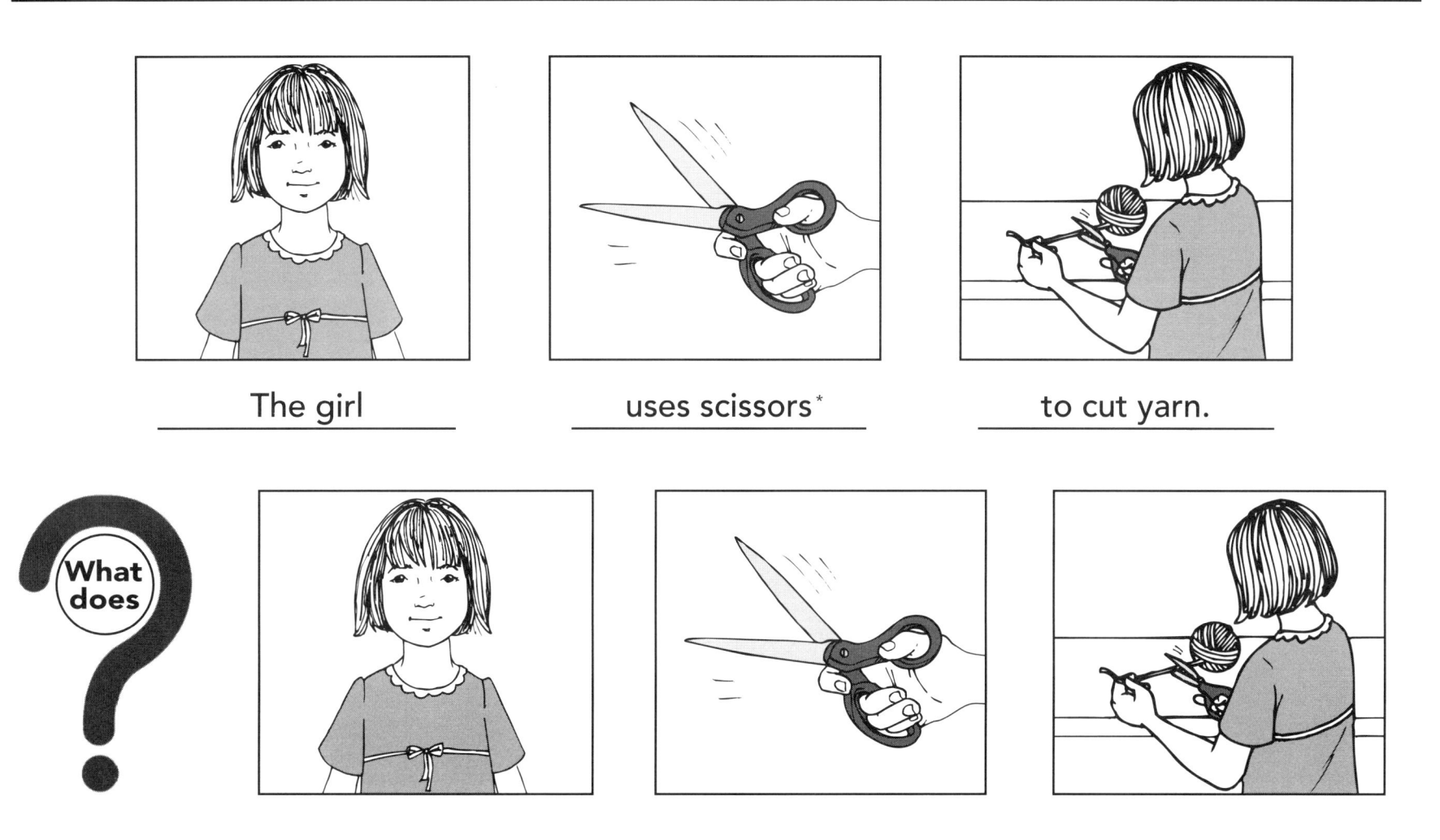

The girl _____ uses scissors* _____ to cut yarn.

What does ... ?

What Questions
No-Glamour Question Structure: Wh- Questions

101

Copyright © 2008 LinguiSystems, Inc.

20 | * The student may need a cue to drop this noun from the question sequence.

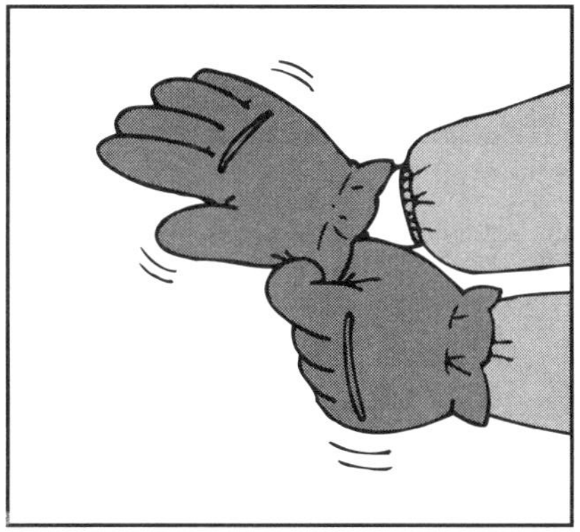

Jack ___ puts on gloves* ___ to play in the snow.

What does

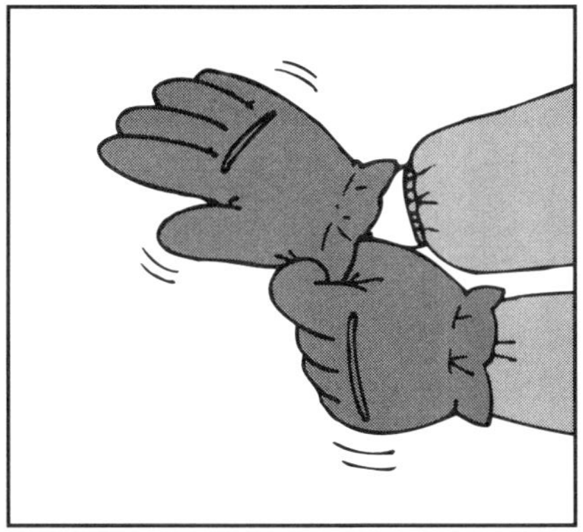

What Questions
No-Glamour Question Structure: Wh- Questions

Unit Review

Write a question that starts with **what** for each picture.

_____ ?

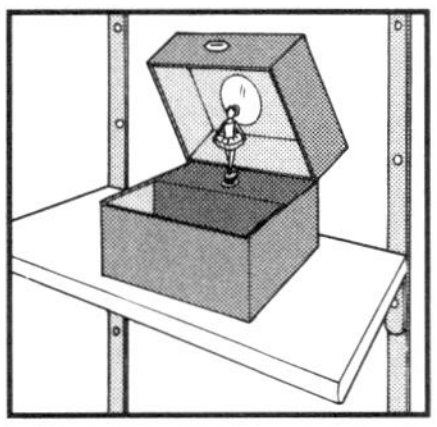

_____

_____

_____

_____

Unit Review, continued

Write a question that starts with **what** for each picture.

_____

_____

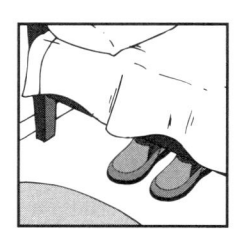

_____

_____

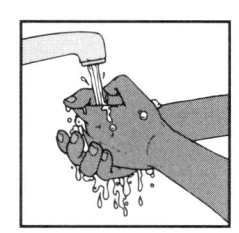

_____

What Questions
No-Glamour Question Structure: Wh- Questions

Unit Review, continued

Write a question that starts with **what** for each picture.

_____

_____

_____

_____

_____

What Questions
No-Glamour Question Structure: Wh- Questions

Unit Review, continued

Write a question that starts with **what** for each picture.

_____

_____

_____

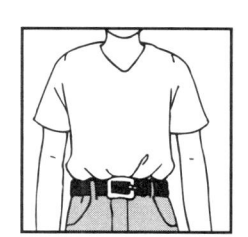

_____

_____

What Questions
No-Glamour Question Structure: Wh- Questions

Why Questions

1. Why is the boy yawning?
2. Why is Aunt Jenny smiling?
3. Why is the door open?
4. Why is the woman wet?
5. Why is the toast black?
6. Why is the lamp on?
7. Why is the ice cream gone?
8. Why are the leaves falling?
9. Why are the deer frightened?
10. Why are the boys and girls standing in line?
11. Why does the tire need air?
12. Why does the catcher wear a mask?
13. Why does the boy get the dog food?
14. Why did the egg break?
15. Why did the little boy cry?
16. Why did the newspaper blow away?
17. Why did the man make a fire?
18. Why should you sleep in a tent?
19. Why should we stand?
20. Why should you call your mom?

Modeling Script:

1. Look at the pictures at the top of the page. Let's point to the pictures and tell what is happening. **The man is drinking water because he is hot.**

2. Now look at the pictures at the bottom of the page. When you see this big question mark, you start with the question word inside the circle. This word is **why**.

3. Now let's ask the whole question while we point to each picture. **Why is the man drinking water?**

4. Now let's write the words under each picture. Remember, a written question ends with a question mark.

1

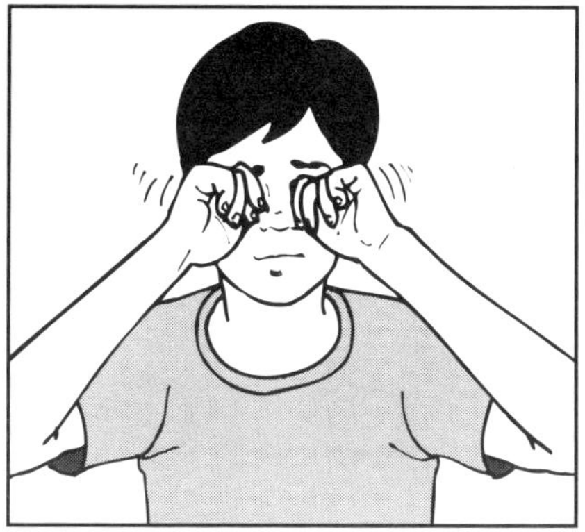

The boy | is yawning | because he is tired.

Why?

Why Questions
No-Glamour Question Structure: Wh- Questions

Aunt Jenny _____ is smiling _____ because she is happy.

Why?

Why Questions
No-Glamour Question Structure: Wh- Questions

The door / is open / because he is leaving.

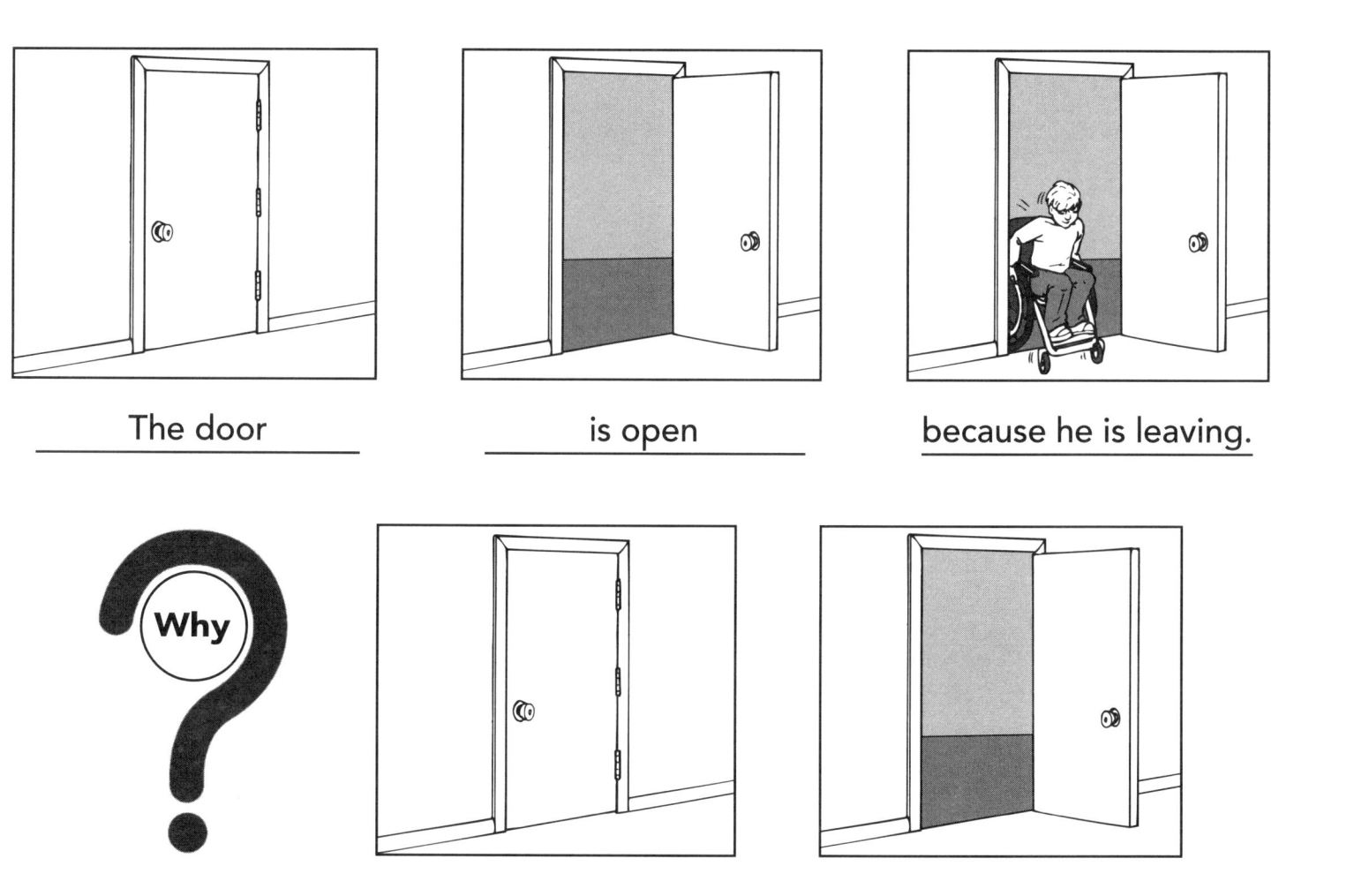

Why?

4

The woman | is wet | because it is raining.

Why?

Why Questions
No-Glamour Question Structure: Wh- Questions

Copyright © 2008 LinguiSystems, Inc.

111

The toast ___ is black ___ because it burned.

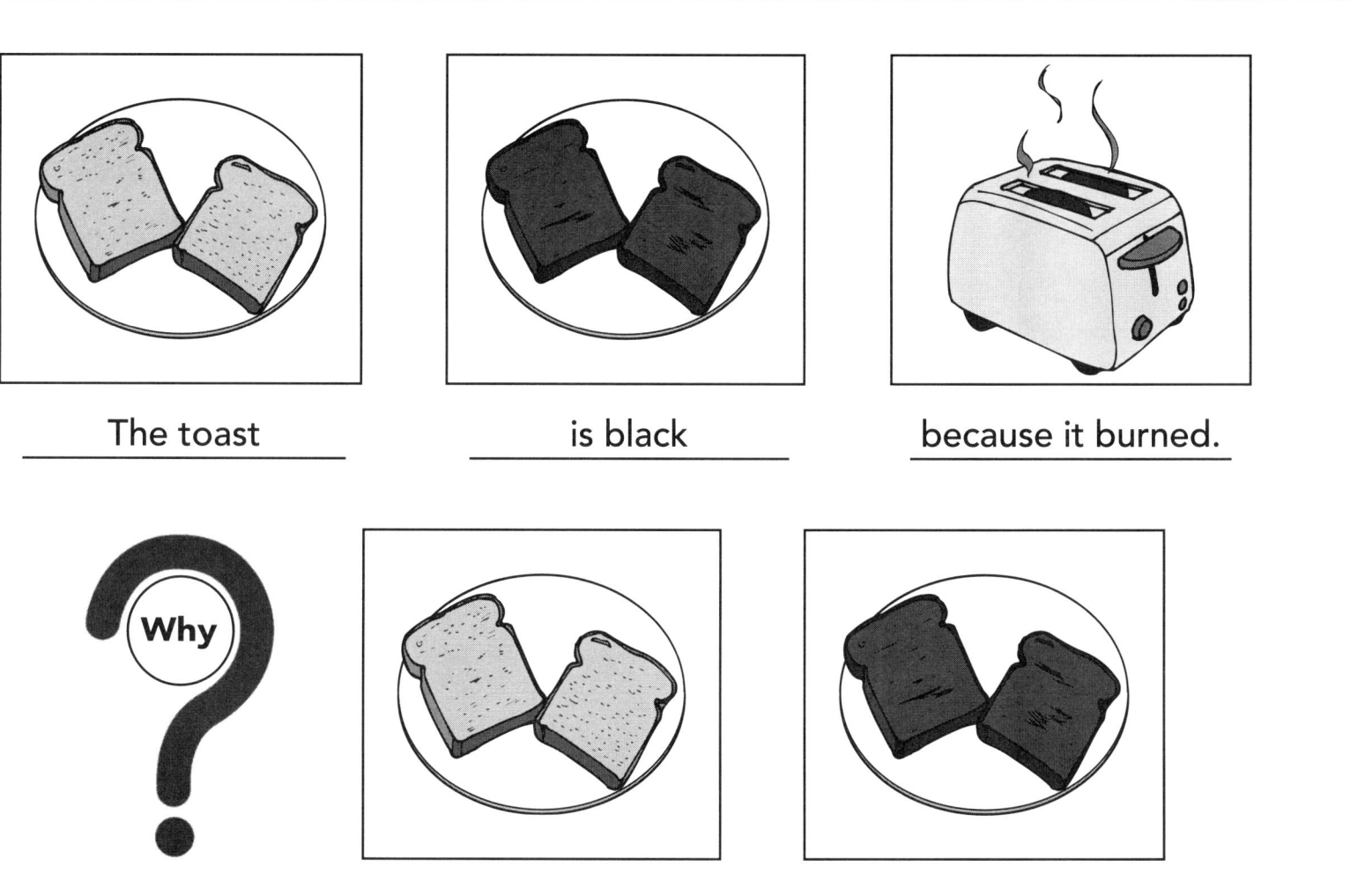

Why?

Why Questions

The lamp   is on   because it is dark.

Why?

7

The ice cream 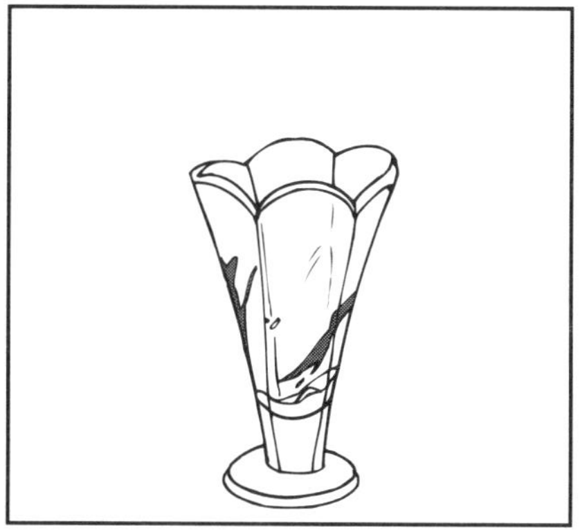 _____ is gone 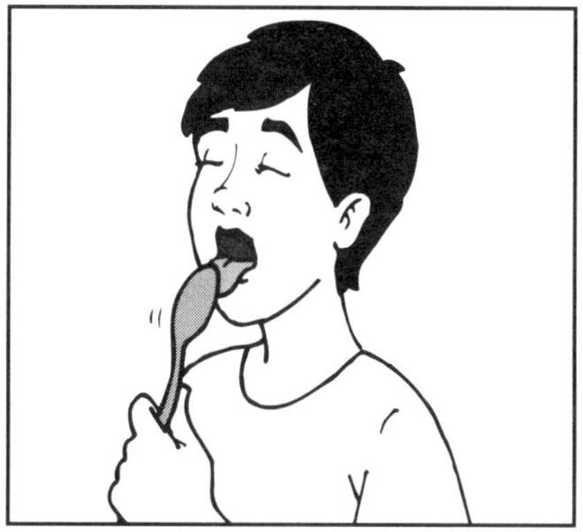 _____ because he ate it.

Why?

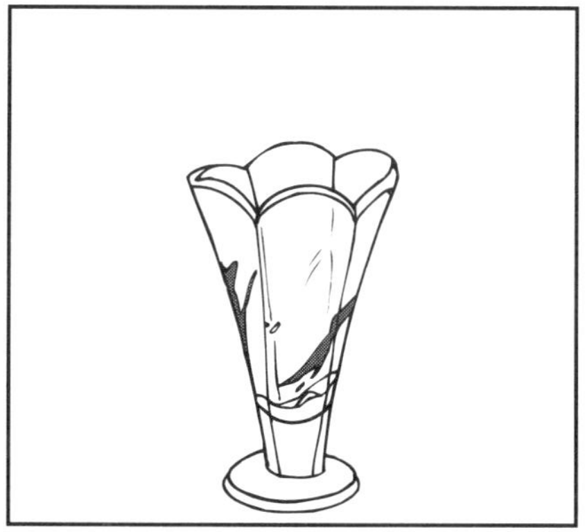

The leaves are falling because it is autumn.

Why?

The deer are frightened because of the fire.

Why?

10

The boys and girls  are standing in line  to ride the go-karts.

Why?

Why Questions
No-Glamour Question Structure: Wh- Questions

Why does...?

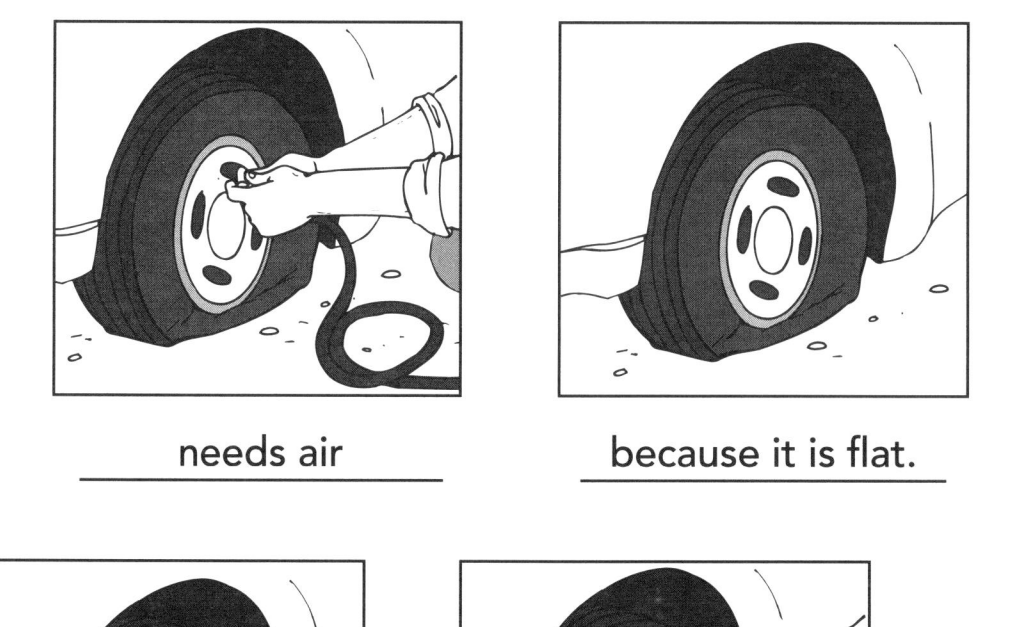

The tire needs air because it is flat.

12

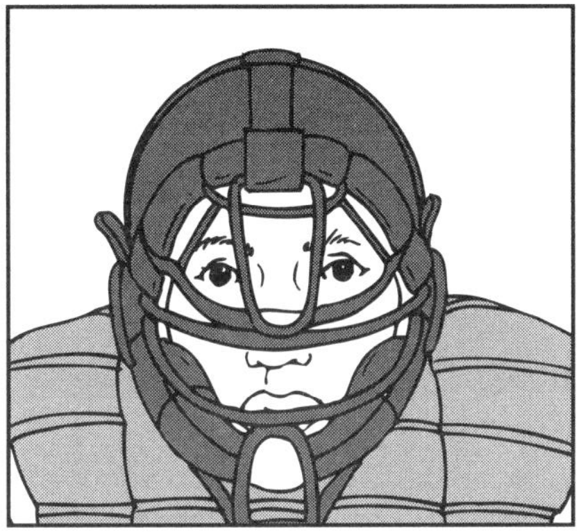

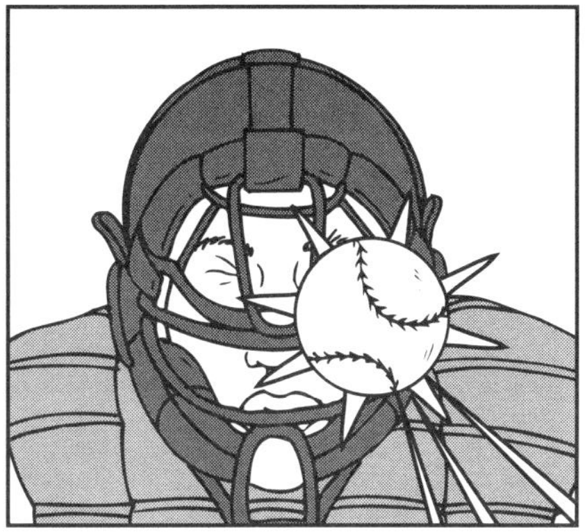

The catcher wears a mask to protect his face.

Why does

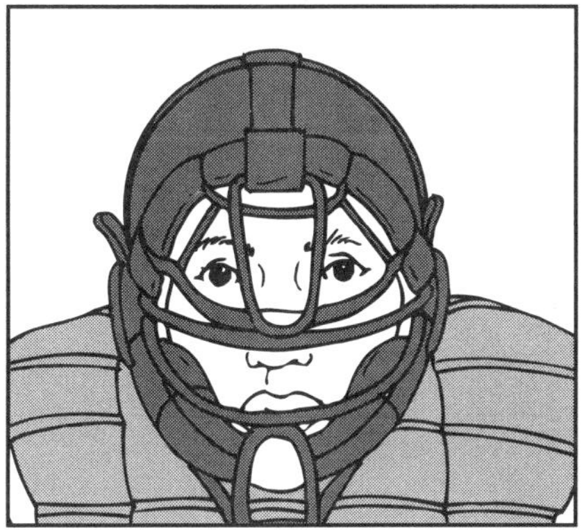

Why Questions
No-Glamour Question Structure: Wh- Questions

13

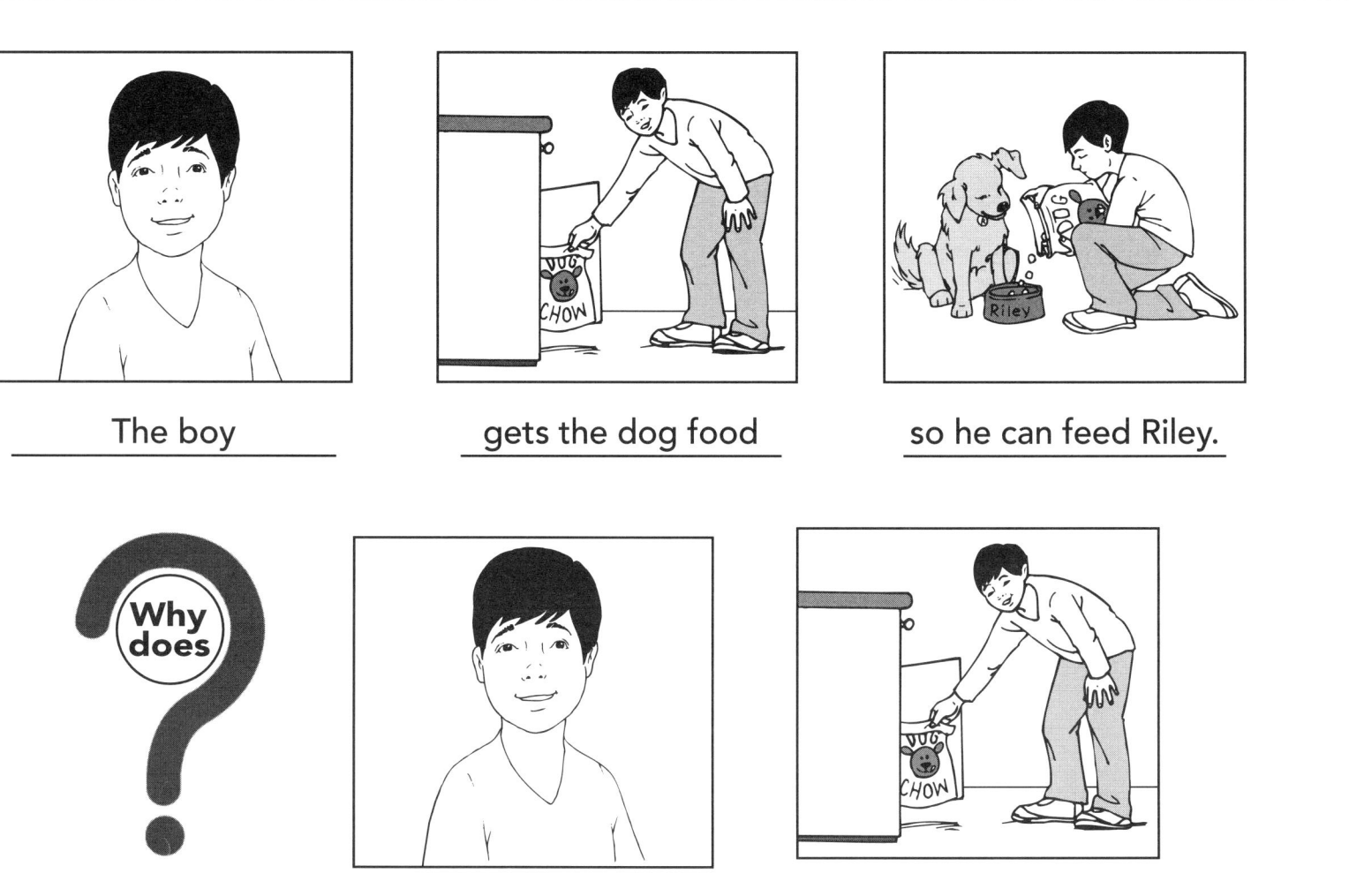

The boy gets the dog food so he can feed Riley.

Why does ?

120

Why Questions
No-Glamour Question Structure: Wh- Questions

Copyright © 2008 LinguiSystems, Inc.

Why did

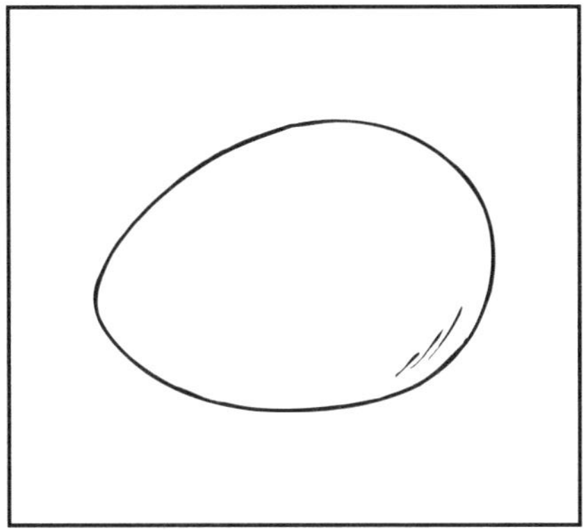

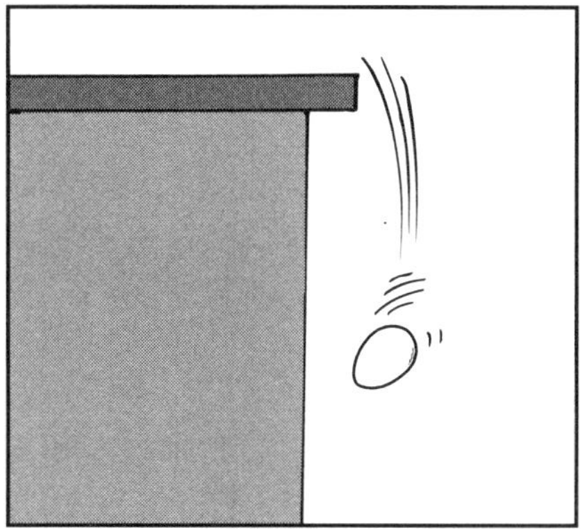

The egg _____ broke _____ because it fell.

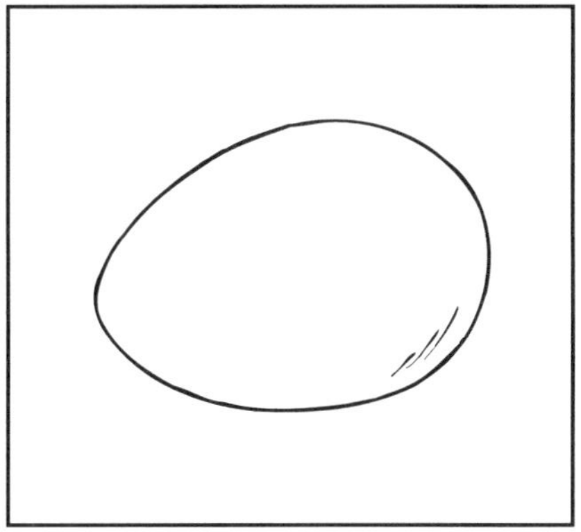

15

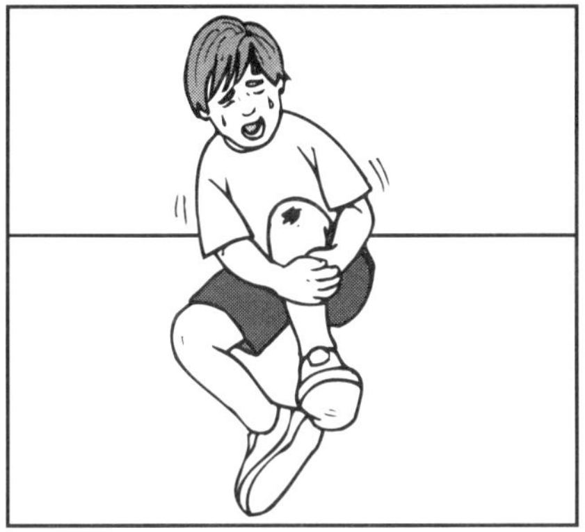

The little boy ___ cried ___ because he fell down.

Why did ?

The newspaper blew away because it is windy.

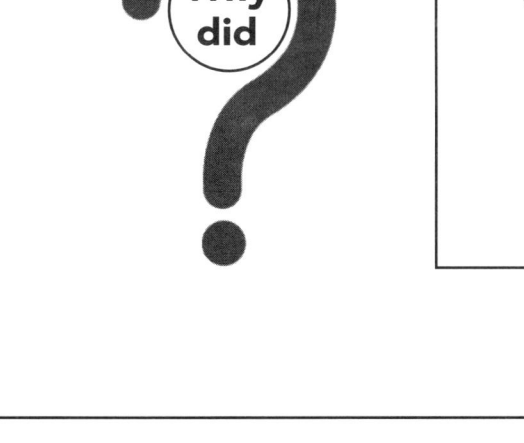

Why did

The man _____ made a fire _____ because he was cold.

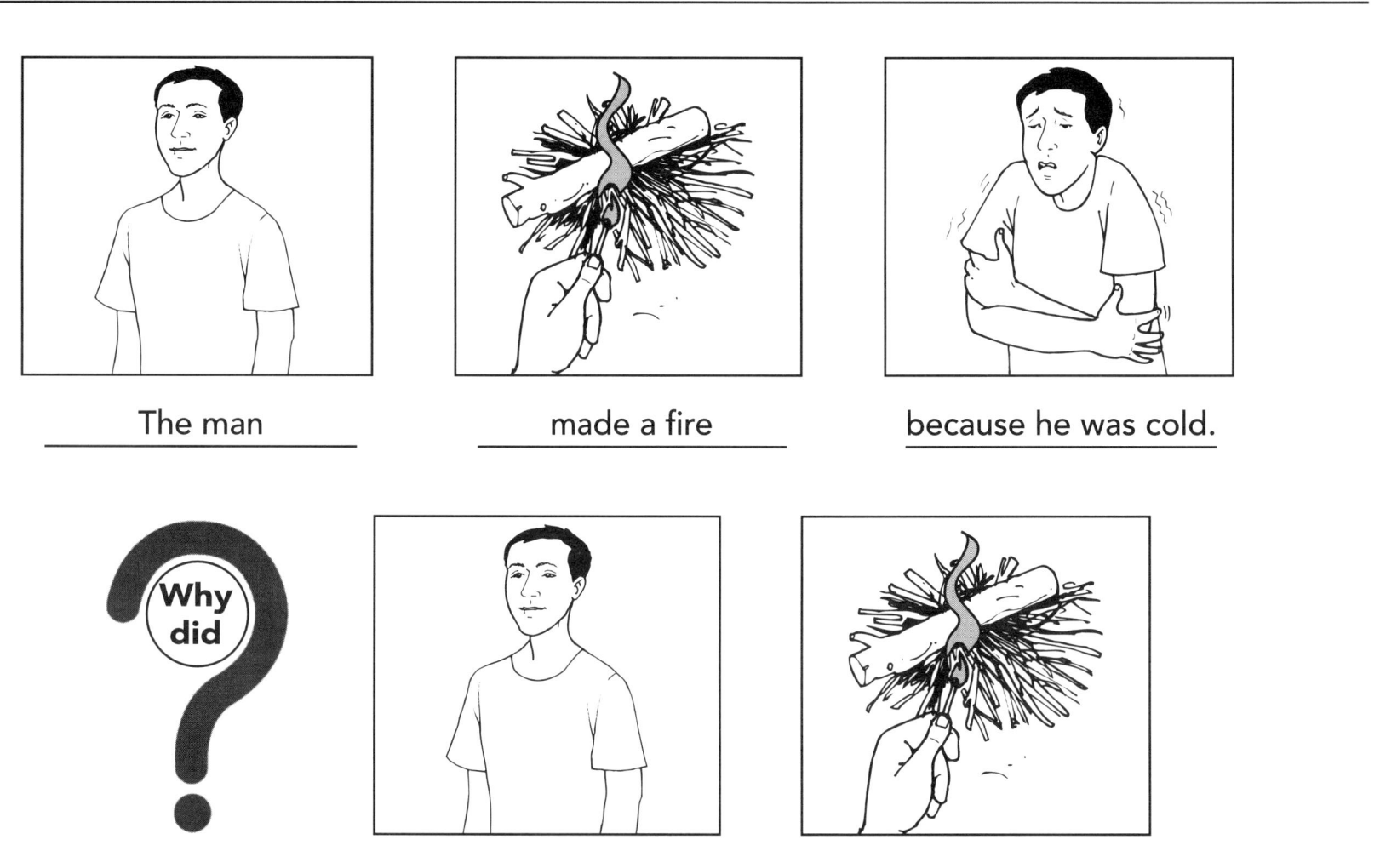

Why did ?

18

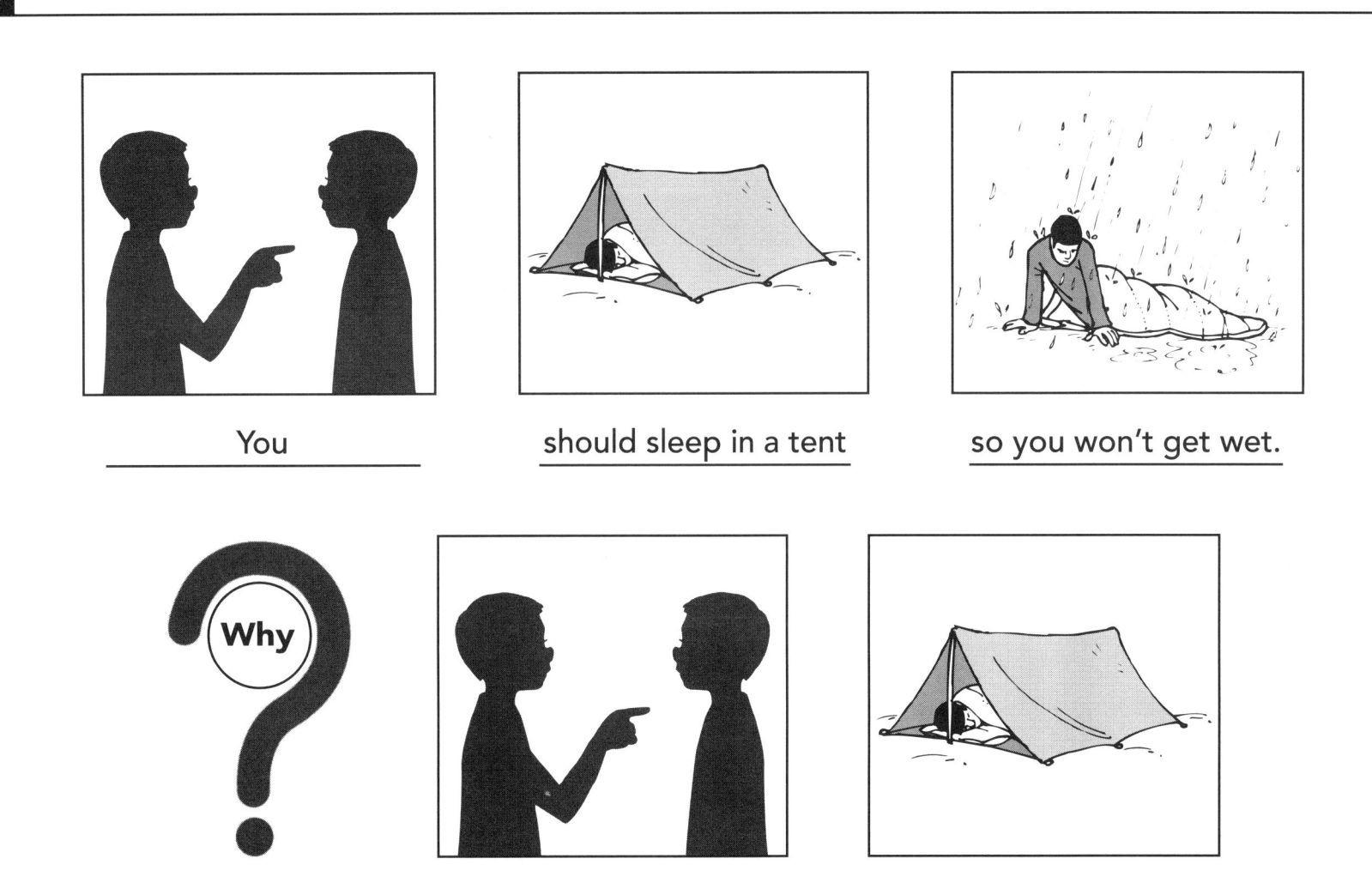

You ___ should sleep in a tent ___ so you won't get wet.

19

We _____ should stand _____ so the women can sit.

Why?

Why Questions
No-Glamour Question Structure: Wh- Questions

20

You  _____ should call your mom  _____ so she doesn't worry.

Why?

Why Questions
No-Glamour Question Structure: Wh- Questions

Unit Review

Write a question that starts with **why** for each picture.

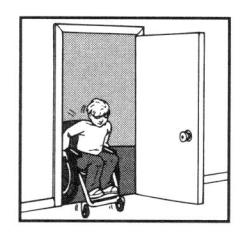

_____ ?

_____

_____

_____

_____

Unit Review, continued

Write a question that starts with **why** for each picture.

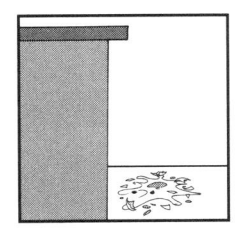

Unit Review, continued

Write a question that starts with **why** for each picture.

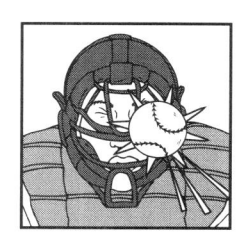

_____

_____

_____

_____

_____

Unit Review, continued

Write a question that starts with **why** for each picture.

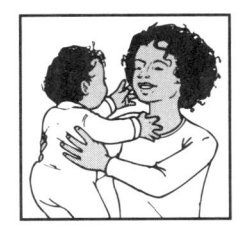

Why Questions
No-Glamour Question Structure: Wh- Questions

How Questions

1. How does a flower smell?
2. How does a siren sound?
3. How does a lemon taste?
4. How does a pillow feel?
5. How does a bird pick up a worm?
6. How does a carpenter cut wood?
7. How do you unlock a door?
8. How do you draw a straight line?
9. How do I dig a hole?
10. How did Ben put the car together?
11. How did the squirrel get in the house?
12. How did the baseball player win the game?
13. How did Mr. Santos reach the ceiling?
14. How did Gina find the campsite?
15. How did Mrs. Watson go downtown?
16. How can you fix torn paper?
17. How can you put out a fire?
18. How can we save gasoline?
19. How can you pay for groceries?
20. How can you make popcorn?

Modeling Script:

1. Look at the pictures at the top of the page. Let's point to the pictures and tell what is happening. **The bride looks beautiful.**

2. Now look at the pictures at the bottom of the page. When you see this big question mark, you start with the question word inside the circle. This word is **how**.

3. Now let's ask the whole question while we point to each picture. **How does the bride look?**

4. Now let's write the words under each picture. Remember, a written question ends with a question mark.

1

A flower _____ smells sweet.

How does?

How Questions
No-Glamour Question Structure: Wh- Questions

2

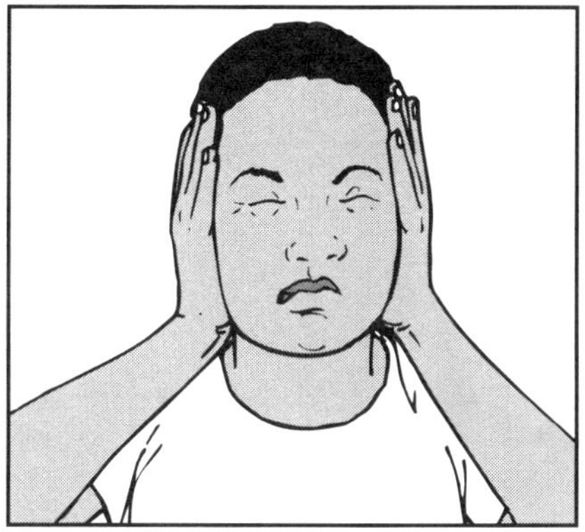

A siren   sounds loud.

How does ?

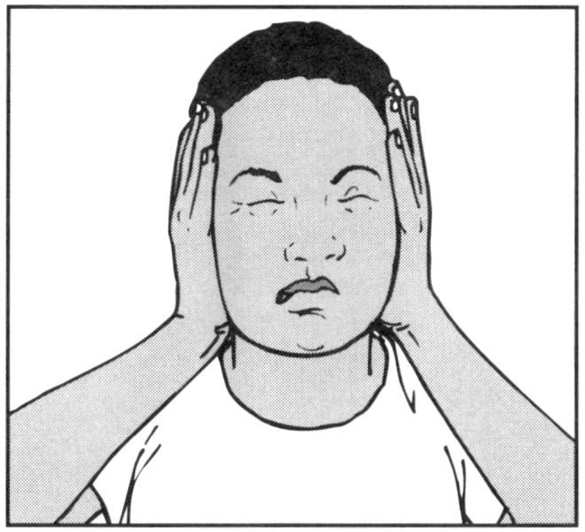

How Questions
No-Glamour Question Structure: Wh- Questions

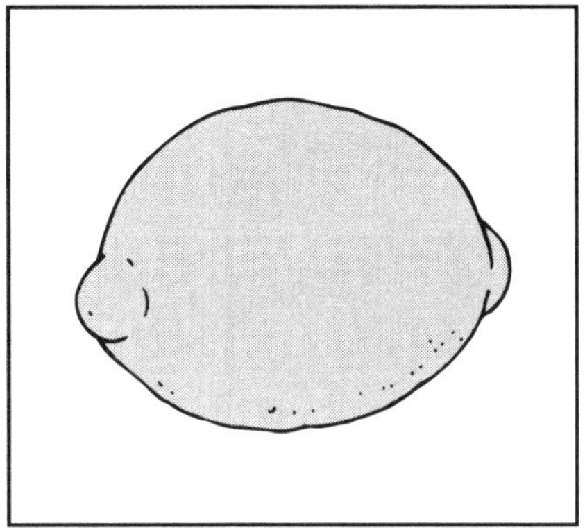

A lemon _____ tastes sour.

How does ?

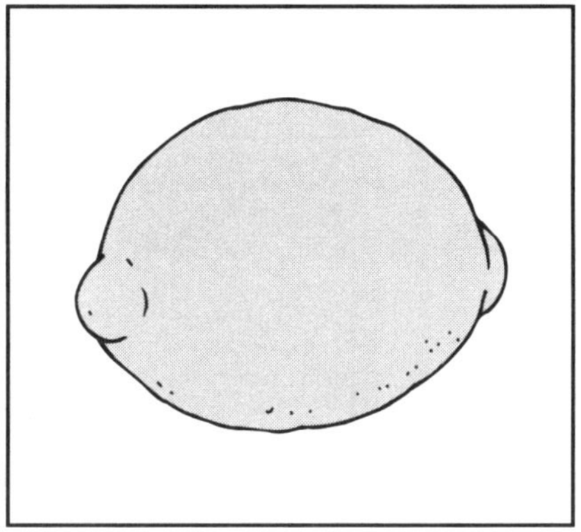

4

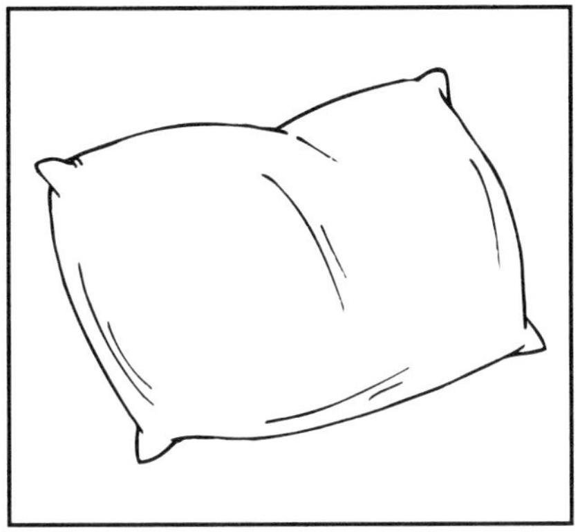

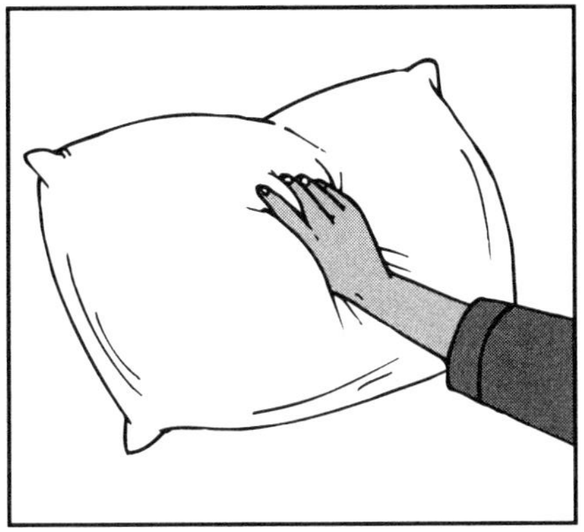

A pillow _____ feels soft. _____

How does

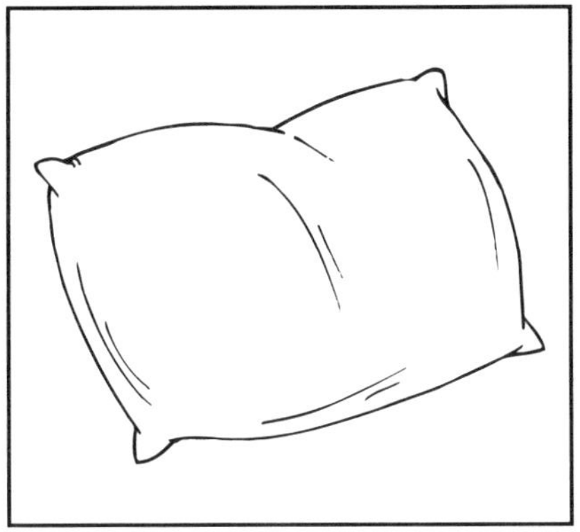

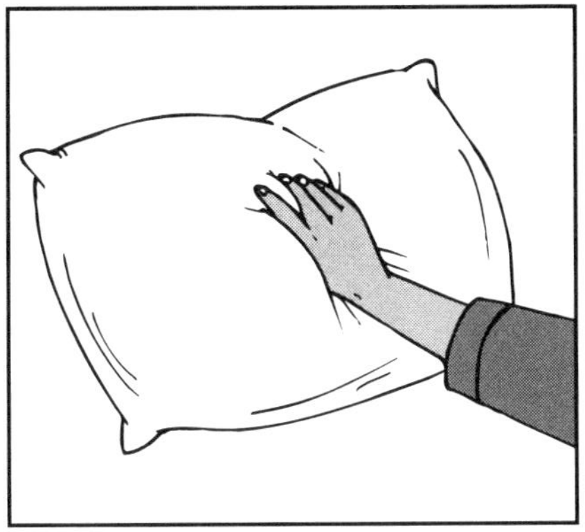

5

A bird    picks up a worm    with its beak.

How does ?

How Questions
No-Glamour Question Structure: Wh- Questions

137

A carpenter 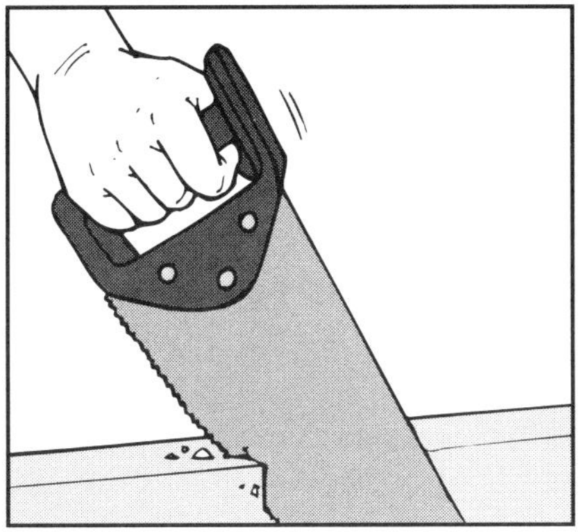 — **cuts wood**  — **with a saw.**

How does ?

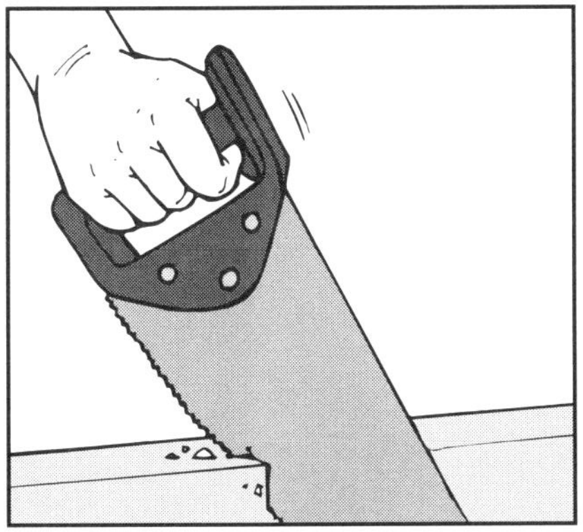

How Questions
No-Glamour Question Structure: Wh- Questions

Copyright © 2008 LinguiSystems, Inc.

7

You — unlock a door — with a key.

How do ?

How do You draw a straight line with a ruler.

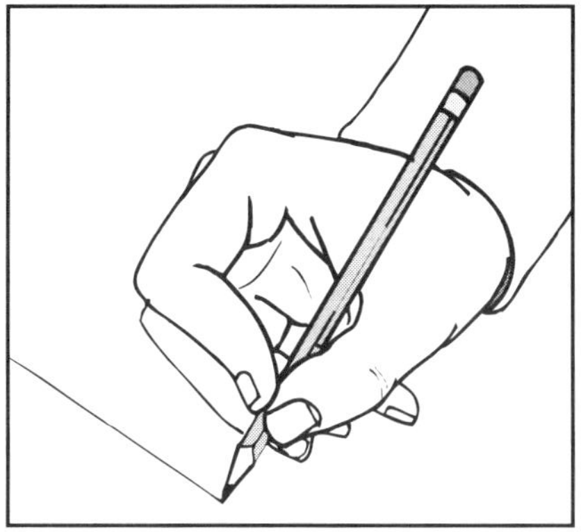

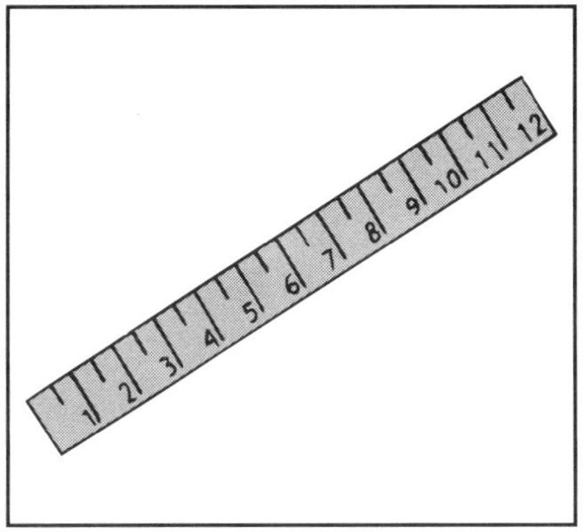

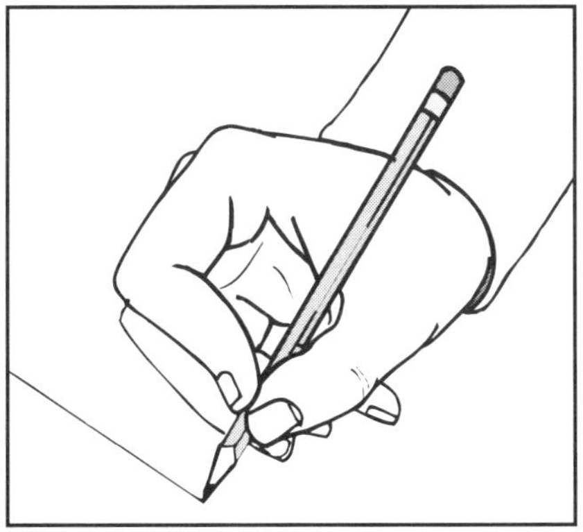

I dig a hole with a shovel.

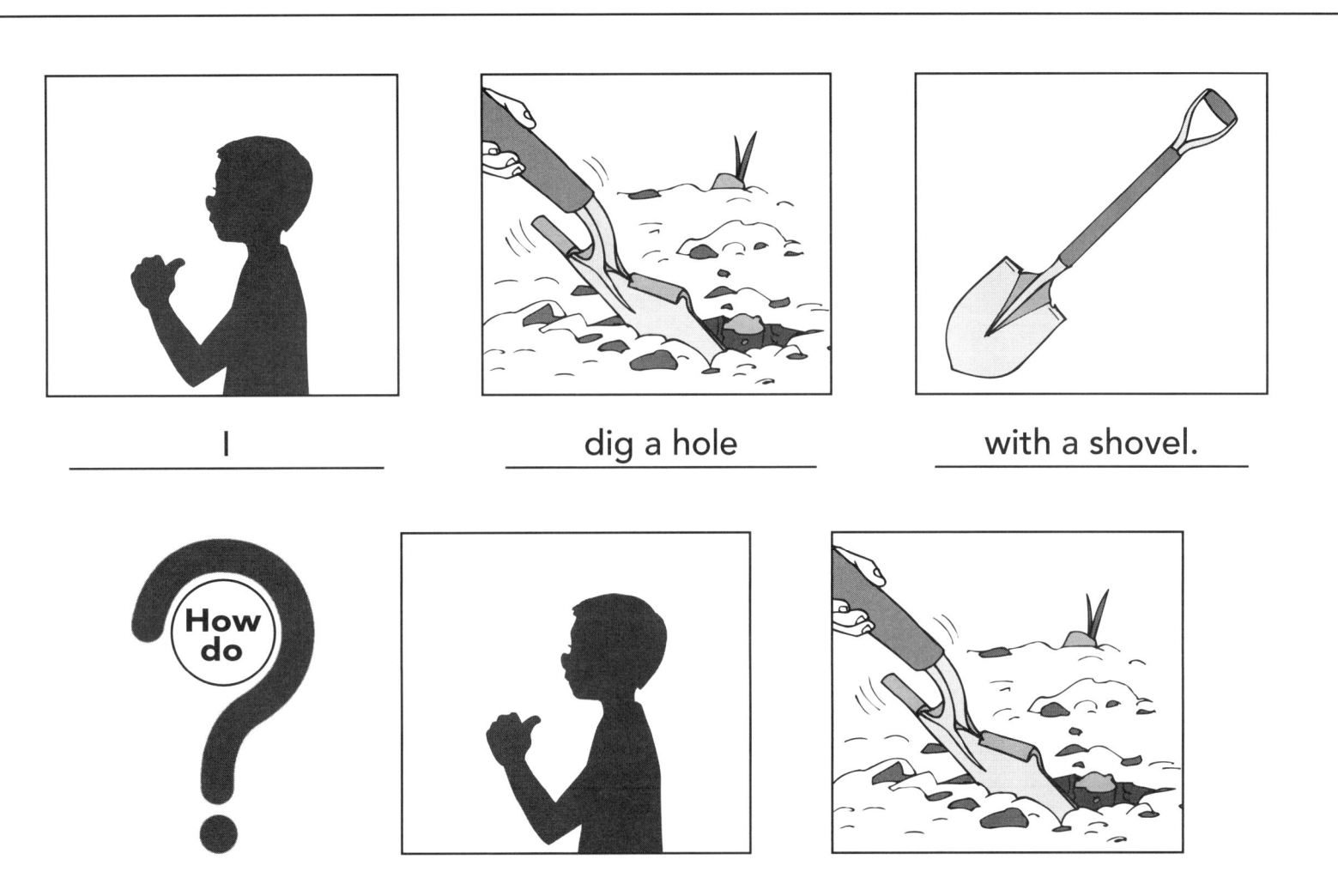

How do ?

How Questions

Ben  _____ put the car together  _____ with glue.

How did _____ ?

The squirrel  got in the house  through the chimney.

How did

12 Remind your student to use the picture cues to form the question as this activity does not follow the normal pattern.

How did

The baseball player   hit a home run   to win the game.

How Questions
No-Glamour Question Structure: Wh- Questions

13 Remind your student to use the picture cues to form the question as this activity does not follow the normal pattern.

Mr. Santos — stood on a ladder — to reach the ceiling.

How did ?

How Questions
No-Glamour Question Structure: Wh- Questions

14 Remind your student to use the picture cues to form the question as this activity does not follow the normal pattern.

Gina   used a map   to find the campsite.

How did

How Questions
No-Glamour Question Structure: Wh- Questions

15

Mrs. Watson _____ went downtown _____ on a bus.

How did _____ ?

How Questions
No-Glamour Question Structure: Wh- Questions

16

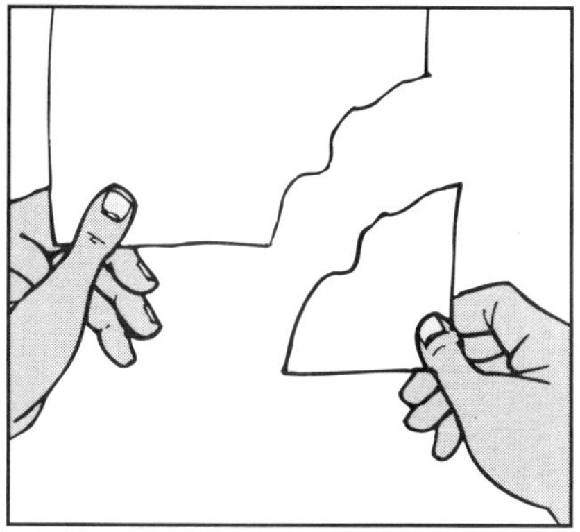

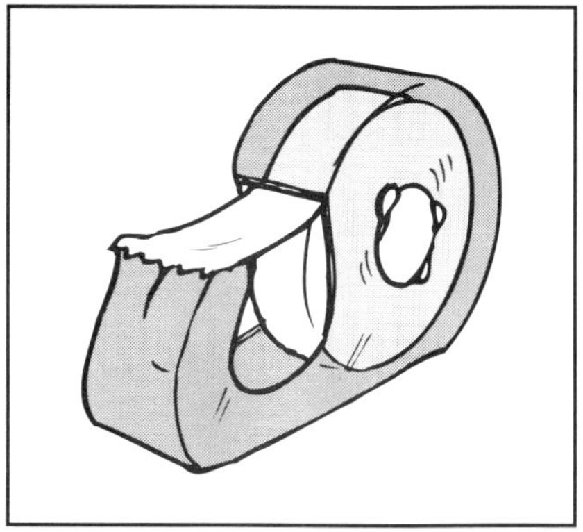

You ___ can fix torn paper ___ with tape.

How can ___?

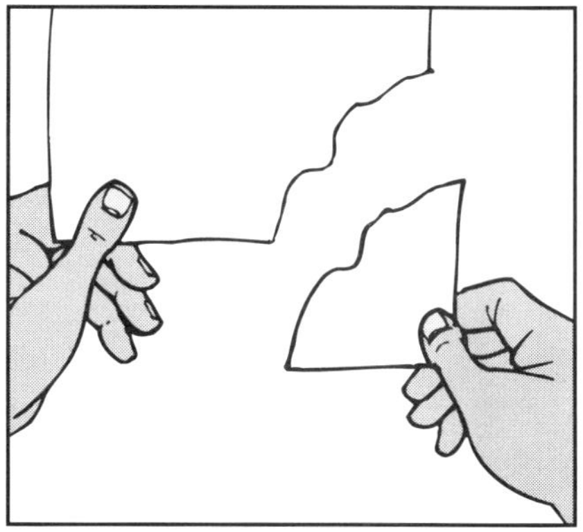

How Questions
No-Glamour Question Structure: Wh- Questions

17

You  _____ can put out a fire  _____ with water.

How can ?

18

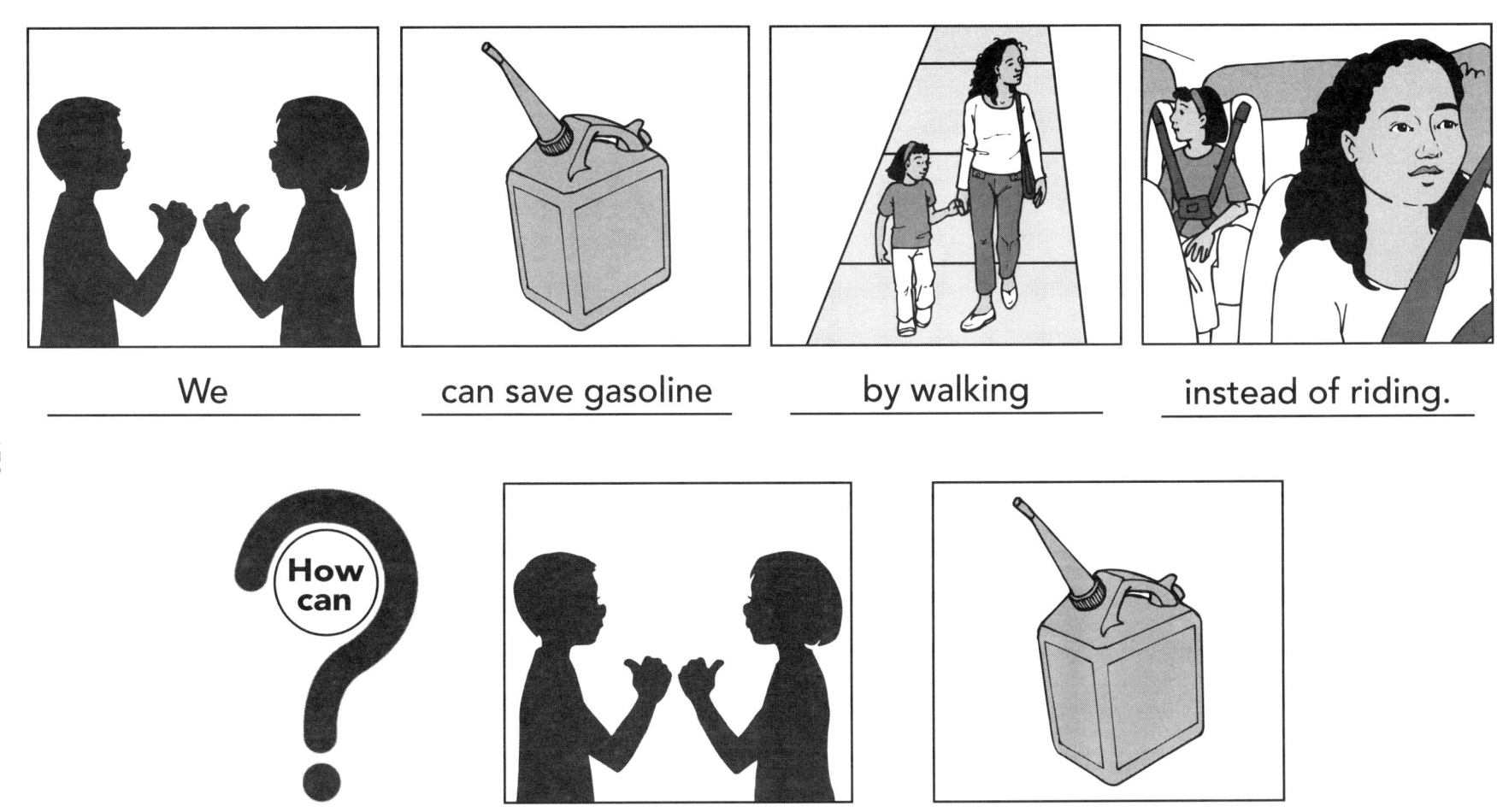

We ___can save gasoline___ ___by walking___ ___instead of riding.___

How can ?

How Questions
No-Glamour Question Structure: Wh- Questions

You | can pay for groceries | with cash | or with a credit card.

How can

20

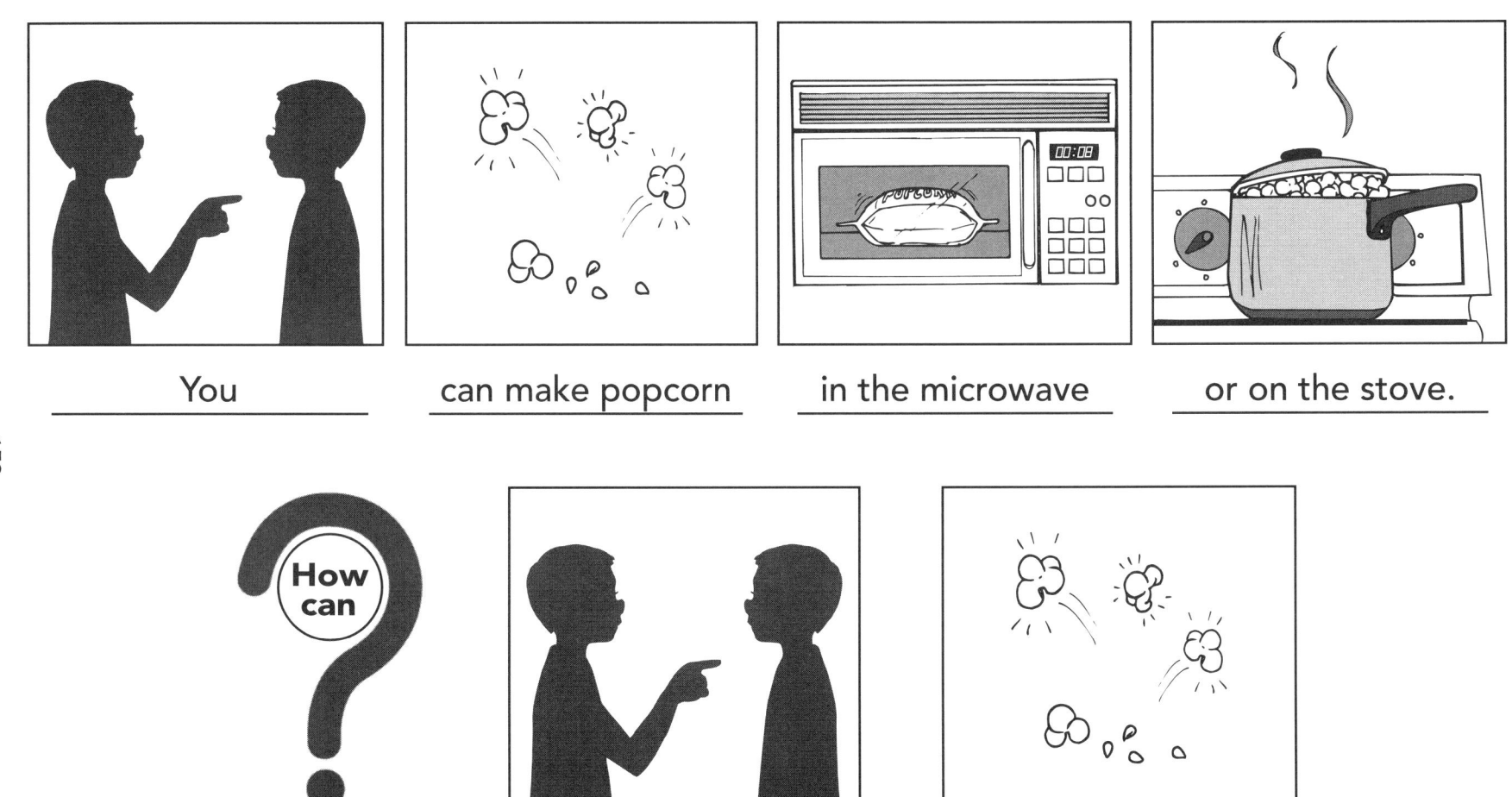

You can make popcorn in the microwave or on the stove.

How can

Unit Review

Write a question that starts with **how** for each picture.

_____?

_____

_____

_____

_____

Unit Review, continued

Write a question that starts with **how** for each picture.

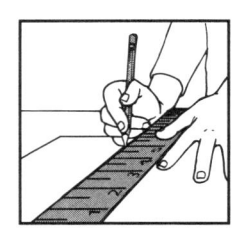

_____

_____

_____

_____

_____

How Questions
No-Glamour Question Structure: Wh- Questions

Unit Review, continued

Write a question that starts with **how** for each picture.

_____

_____

_____

_____

_____

How Questions
No-Glamour Question Structure: Wh- Questions

Unit Review, *continued*

Write a question that starts with **how** for each picture.

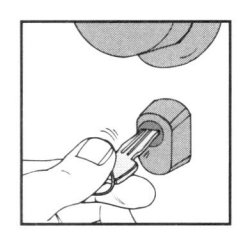

_____

_____

_____

_____

_____

Wrap-Up

Ask four questions about this picture. Begin your questions with the question words listed. The first one is done for you.

Kevin is swinging.

Who is swinging?

What

Where

Why

Wrap-Up, continued

Ask four questions about this picture. Begin your questions with the question words listed.

The giraffe is chewing leaves.

What _____

Where _____

Why _____

How _____

Wrap-Up, continued

Ask four questions about this picture. Begin your questions with the question words listed.

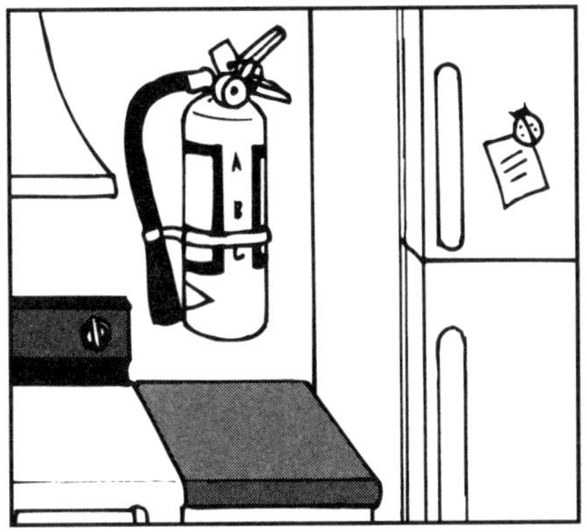

A fire extinguisher is in the kitchen.

What

Where

Why

When

Wrap-Up, continued

Ask four questions about this picture. Begin your questions with the question words listed.

Max goes in his doghouse when it rains.

Where _____

When _____

Why _____

What _____

Wrap-Up, continued

Ask four questions about this picture. Begin your questions with the question words listed.

Stan put the marbles in the jar.

Where _____

What _____

Who _____

Why _____

No-Glamour Question Structure: Wh- Questions

Wrap-Up, continued

Ask four questions about this picture. Begin your questions with the question words listed.

Construction workers wear hardhats at work.

Who ___

What ___

Why ___

When ___

Wrap-Up, continued

Ask four questions about this picture. Begin your questions with the question words listed.

The fisherman cast his line into the lake.

Who _____

Where _____

What _____

Why _____

Wrap-Up, continued

Ask four questions about this picture. Begin your questions with the question words listed.

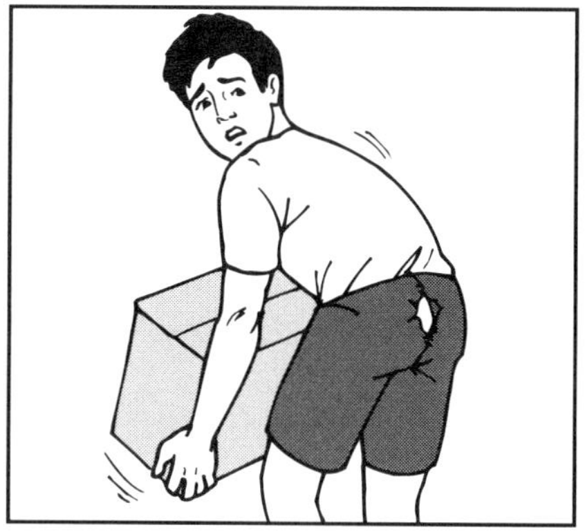

Erik ripped his pants when he bent over.

How _____

When _____

What _____

Why _____

Wrap-Up, *continued*

Ask four questions about this picture. Begin your questions with the question words listed.

The children will hide while Peggy counts.

Who

What

When

Why

Wrap-Up, continued

Ask four questions about this picture. Begin your questions with the question words listed.

If you knock over the pins, you will win a prize.

What _____

How _____

Who _____

Where _____